Life from Scratch

LIFE FROM
Family Traditions

SCRATCH

That Start with You

Vanessa Lachey

WITH DINA GACHMAN

HarperOne
An Imprint of HarperCollins*Publishers*

HarperCollins books may be purchased for educational, business, or sales promotional use. For information, please email the Special Markets Department at SPsales@harpercollins.com.

FIRST EDITION

Designed by Kris Tobiassen for Matchbook Digital, LLC

Photography:
Courtesy of the author: pages 62, 66 (bottom), 117, 146
Scott Clark: pages 42, 44, 82, 84, 98, 100, 102, 103, 104
Justin Coit: pages ii–iii, x, 5, 8, 10, 17, 22, 29, 30, 32, 35, 36, 37, 39, 40, 41, 46, 48, 49, 53, 56, 60, 63, 76, 77, 79, 94, 106, 108, 110, 112, 114, 122 (excluding TV screen), 126, 128, 133, 137, 142, 145, 154, 157, 158, 161, 163, 164, 166, 170, 173, 174, 176, 179, 183, 184, 187, 189, 191, 193, 194, 199, 203, 204–5, 208, 211, 212, 215, 216
Paul Cook: page 27
Rhonda Dent: pages 25, 67, 68, 116
Lex Gallegos for Scott Clark Photography: pages 50, 70, 72, 73
Jennifer Hochstadt: page 6
Joyce Park: page 92
Stuart Ruckman: page 26
Justine Ungaro: pages 88, 118, 121, 130
Megan Welker: pages vi, 64, 66 (top), 152
© Dmytro Aksonov/iStock/Getty Images: page 122 (TV screen)
© klenova/iStock/Getty Images: page 138

Library of Congress Cataloging-in-Publication Data has been applied for.

ISBN 978-0-06-303176-0

21 22 23 24 25 TC 10 9 8 7 6 5 4 3 2 1

To my loving husband, Nick, and our
three beautiful babies, Camden, Brooklyn, and Phoenix:
everything good in my life is because of *you*.

Contents

Summer

Fall

Winter

Introduction

My family is *everything* to me. My husband, Nick, and my three children, Camden, Brooklyn, and Phoenix, have filled my life with more love than I thought possible—and more messes than I'd like to admit! My days, like for most families, are a nonstop juggling act of kid extracurriculars, working, whipping up a healthy (or—let's be real—quick) dinner, and the occasional but essential date night with my husband.

When I became a wife and then a mom, I remember continually seeking advice about how to handle the beautiful chaos that is life. I sought guidance from friends, siblings, and coworkers because I didn't have a mom by my side to pass down motherly wisdom. How should I handle an irate toddler while I'm trying to bake the perfect chicken enchiladas—all while holding on tightly to my sanity and even more tightly to my glass of wine?

Here are the facts. My mother disappeared from my life when I was nine years old. Long story short (which, by the way, is a phrase that drives Nick crazy, since I like to talk and my stories are rarely short): It was August of 1990, and the Gulf War was just beginning. My dad was on active duty in the air force, and my brother and I were living in Turkey with my mom and stepdad, who was also in the military. I guess it's safe to say that my mom had a type. Anyway, one day I was in my fourth-grade classroom, and an announcement came over the loud-speaker asking us to drop to our knees and pray for our military. We were told we were getting evacuated back to the United States for safety while our military family members stayed behind. We boarded a cargo plane back to America.

Back in the US, my mom ended up on my dad and stepmom's doorstep. My dad was away serving our country, so my stepmom, Donna, answered the door, and my mom asked her to take care of me and my brother until she could get back on her feet. Donna agreed (I mean, what was she supposed to do?), and after that, my mom showed up once a week for the next couple of weeks to take me and my brother to lunch. By the third week, she was MIA.

There were no letters from my mom in the weeks that followed. No calls. My dad lived in fear that my mom would show up and take me and my brother back, since she had legal custody. Perhaps for this reason my stepmom kept her distance emotionally. But my mother never came back. I secretly lived in hope that one day she'd show up and I would have that role model I always wanted. She did show up once, when I was in sixth grade, and she took me and my brother to see *The Bodyguard*, starring Whitney Houston. Going to that movie was the last time I would truly feel connected to her and loved by her. The main song from the film, "I Will Always Love You," haunted me for years! When I started acting, in my twenties, and I needed to cry for a part, I would sing that song in my head.

My mom disappeared again until one day in 1998, right after I won Miss Teen USA. I was eighteen years old, and I was at my grandmother's house, in Florida, when the phone rang. After the very first "Hello?" I recognized my mom's voice. I nearly dropped the phone in shock. The sound of her voice after all those years paralyzed me, and I could barely breathe. After some awkward greetings, she said she wanted to see me. Regardless of how nervous I was, she *was* my mom, so I agreed. I told her I'd be in North Carolina later that summer and that we could meet then, since she was living near there. And that was that. We hung up, and I went back to being Miss Teen USA, with a future date to see a mother I had dreamed about being with for almost a decade.

Later that summer, the big day came, and there she was, standing at my hotel room door. As soon as I saw her I realized how terribly I had missed her (despite everything!), and I suddenly hoped that *this* was the beginning of a "normal" relationship—one in which I had a mom who would love me and answer all my questions about life, love, guys, fashion, our family history, secret recipes, her amazing jewelry. You know, typical mother-daughter stuff.

It didn't take long for me to realize that we wouldn't be sitting down for deep and meaningful life lessons anytime soon. She hadn't traveled to my hotel room to congratulate me. She wanted to know how much money I had won as Miss Teen USA. She asked if I had won a car.

I was crushed. It was everything I had feared, deep down. You might think I'm crazy, but I did end up giving her money. I gave her pretty much everything I'd won, because even at that age, I felt I would always regret not helping her out, and based on our history I knew it would be the last time I would ever see her. And it was. That was the end of my dream of having a perfect mom come back and save the day—and save *me*. I would have to be my own guide through life.

Eventually I pulled myself together, wiped away the tears, and got back to building a life. I vowed to make it special, make it my own. I came to realize that experiences like this wouldn't break me. I mean, I had already survived a lot. Like having to ask my dad how to use tampons. Talk about mortifying! And wearing a white dress to a friend's wedding (because no one told me not to) and then being completely embarrassed when the caterers kept congratulating me because they thought I was the bride. I had to learn to cook on my own and discover ways to be a great parent despite not having had a loving mother who led by example.

Many of the women I look to, like Ayesha Curry, Reese Witherspoon, Kate Hudson, and Rashida Jones, *do* have a strong female presence in their lives. I admit I get a little jealous when I see Ayesha's mom making her bone broth when she's sick, Reese's mom passing down all her Southern secrets, Kate's mom offering loving advice for her lasting, happy partnership, and Rashida's supportive relationship with her mom who is her biggest fan. But I'm also happy for them, because it's a beautiful thing. Some of my friends have moms who taught them how to sew homemade Halloween costumes or handed them a secret recipe book that's been in the family for generations, and I love hearing all of their stories and advice. What I've learned is that none of us have picture-perfect pasts, and we are all truly making it up as we go along. But our messy pasts don't define our futures. They may influence them, but it's up to us to make our lives just that—*ours*. Perfectly imperfect.

I've tried to turn each challenge in life into an opportunity, and, as it turned out, I have *loved* creating new family traditions. I didn't realize that I had been creating a "life from scratch" until a few years ago. It all started with a dish I absolutely love, chicken adobo. This is a Filipino recipe, and my mom is a Filipina, so hello, Freud! I found comfort in this meal from my very early childhood, a time when I'd sit on my mom's lap and eat the salty, savory dish. One Christmas a few years after I got married, I was standing in the kitchen with my friend Lauren, working on my chicken adobo. Lauren assumed I had learned the recipe from my mom and asked if she had passed it down to me. Since that was a hard no, I explained that it was a dish I had been googling and experimenting with for a few years, eventually tweaking it to make it my own. That's when she said the words that would shift my thinking forever:

"Oh, so this tradition is starting with you . . ."

Her words had such an impact that I almost needed to hear them again. *Yes!* She was absolutely right. This tradition started with me, not my mom or anyone else. This was a recipe that my husband and kids would remember and that I could pass on to them, and maybe they'd pass it down to their kids one day. It was an incredible realization.

That's what I hope to share with you in these pages: the feeling that you're creating something unique and special for the ones you love, whether it's a

family Thanksgiving that makes November pure magic, the simple yearly gift-giving custom I share with my best girlfriends, or the date-night tradition Nick and I swear by that helps us stay connected despite endless kid birthday parties, school functions, and long workdays. These traditions mean the world to me and have shown me that I have the power to create the family I *want* to have, not the family I *wish* I'd had. I'm not gonna lie: at times, winging it has been tough, but it has also made me more resilient, more creative, and much more appreciative of the moments that really matter. It has taken me more than a decade to become the "perfect" wife and mom—and yes, I use those quotation marks with a heavy dose of sarcasm. Because none of us can ever be perfect, but we can create lasting memories—like making a cute Valentine's Day treat for our kids each year or starting unique birthday traditions—that make our lives feel if not perfect, then inspiring, happy, and full.

Look: no matter what our background or circumstances may be, as parents and partners and humans, we're all making it up as we go—with the help of girlfriends, guy friends, and maybe even books like this. If you want to make a recipe from this book and add a sprinkle of oregano because it reminds you of your grandmother, go for it! If you want to tweak a holiday decorating idea as a tribute to your best friend, please do—I'd be honored. There's no cookie-cutter way to go through this crazy, beautiful, chaotic life. We all love differently, we all think differently, and we all have to make it work differently. But traditions help bridge our differences and bring us together.

While my hope is that this book entertains you and makes you laugh, I also hope it helps you see that the future is yours to define. And most important, I hope it inspires you to write your own story, create your own traditions, make your own chicken adobo, and find connection through a life shaped, defined, and created by *you*—and shared with those you love.

So here's to living *Life from Scratch* . . . on your own terms.

PART 1

Spring

Nick grew up in Cincinnati, and I remember going to visit his family in early spring one year. It was sixty degrees outside, but everyone was wearing shorts and flip-flops, as if the thermometer read ninety-eight degrees (*wink, wink*). I was freezing, since living in Southern California spoils you when it comes to weather, but Nick explained that in a place like Cincinnati, where it really *is* freezing all winter, people throw off their jackets, slip into sandals, and start celebrating the minute there's a sign that winter is ending and spring is in the air.

That's what spring means to me—a new start, throwing off the old, and the excitement of sunshine and warmer days to come. Spring is jasmine-scented candles, dappled sunshine coming through the kitchen windows, buying fresh flowers for your home. It's an exhale after the chaos and cold of winter. I feel more energized when the days are warmer and the sun goes down later, which might be why most of us are motivated to start working out or cleaning out our garages or getting rid of things we no longer need in the spring.

I hope these spring traditions get you organized, enhance your creativity, and inspire you to toss off your old heavy boots and put on a pair of breezy flip-flops as you celebrate new beginnings. Oh, and good food. Always good food.

CHAPTER 1

Out with the Old

As soon as spring rolls around, I feel the urge to Marie Kondo my bedroom, throw open the windows, and switch out my evergreen-scented winter candles for lighter scents such as gardenia and lemongrass and—one of my favorites—vanilla lavender. A few years ago I saw a professional organizer on a daytime talk show, and some of his ideas transformed the way I organize everything, from my utensils to my candles. Yes, I organize my candles! What can I say? It makes me happy.

The organizer basically said, "Everything has a place." It sounds simple, but most of us leave things scattered around the house, especially when we're continually picking up after kids. He held up a fork and said, "What is this?" The audience members laughed. "Where does it go?" he asked, then answered his own question: "In the kitchen utensil drawer." He was saying that everything has a place, and if you put all the similar things in a designated place, you will always know where things are. You will also know when you need more (or less) of them. And you won't waste time looking for things, since they are in their appropriate *places*.

Right then I decided to organize my candles. I grabbed them from the bedrooms, bathrooms, kitchen, guest room, cabinets—basically all over the house. I couldn't believe how many I had. It was a reality check for me. I now confess: I'm a candle hoarder. After that, I created a special candle cabinet, which saves me from rummaging in cabinets and drawers looking for a new candle. The professional organizer was right: I now know exactly where my candles are—and I know that I don't need to buy a new one for about twenty years.

Not everyone shares my love of spring cleaning and organizing. It's sometimes a struggle to get motivated when you're staring at a messy closet and the phone is ringing and your kids are reminding you that they're bored. But if you think of it as a yearly tradition, one that helps you declutter your life not just physically but mentally as well, it might just become something you look forward to. To quote Marie Kondo, "A dramatic reorganization of the home causes correspondingly dramatic changes in lifestyle and perspective. It is life transforming."

If you're still skeptical (or if you already love spring cleaning and just want a few new tricks to make it feel a little more fun), I have some tried-and-true tips to help you kick-start a yearly ritual that'll make you feel rejuvenated, renewed, and restored.

Get Organized

I know for many of you, getting organized might sound about as fun as a trip to the dentist, but if you look at it as an activity that will help you feel lighter and more Zen, it won't seem so torturous (I swear)! First things first: I'm a label girl. I highly recommend investing in a label maker so you can organize everything from your winter clothes to your holiday decor to your kitchen gear. Jumbled messes and clutter stress me out. Don't get me wrong—I have mini messes and piles all over the place. But the disorder starts to affect my emotional state, and that's why this process is so important to me.

Best Uses for a Label Maker

Snacks: I like to label bins with "Kids' Snacks" so they can grab and go. It makes it easier for parents, plus the kids are learning to be self-sufficient.

Seasonal clothing: Winter sweaters, swimsuits, and so on.

Makeup: Separate lipsticks from eye shadows, concealers, and pencils.

Spices and seasonings: If you store them in glass jars, salt and sugar can look very similar and lead to some interesting mix-ups in the kitchen!

Laundry-room items: Putting everything in labeled bins helps keep the area looking tidy and cleaning products together.

Kids' toys: Use colored label tape and write the toy category or color to help your kids learn reading. For example: I have labeled our toy cars by color in separate bins. The kids have fun and can always "find the blue truck"!

Kids' clothing: Especially baby clothes, which they seem to grow out of within a week! I like labeling sizes for babies and clothes type for older kids.

Socks and T-shirts: This helps Nick keep organized, because we can separate things like nice crewneck shirts from concert tees and dress socks from sport socks.

Jeans: Skinny, high-waisted, boot-cut, and so on.

Travel items: For example, "Camden's Pajamas, Socks & Boxers" is the label for one travel zipper bag.

Seasonal decor: This seems obvious, but even more detailed labels help. For example, "Santa Photos with Kids." Or "Kitchen Christmas Decor" for that dinner party that you want to be festive.

When I thought back to the time when my love of organizing started, I realized I've been into labeling from a young age. Did you ever make mixtapes or CDs (remember those?) of your favorite songs? I made one of slow jams, another of love songs, and another I played when I was working out. I have memories of my mom labeling VHS tapes, too. The tapes came with stickers, and she would label each movie and then organize them not just alphabetically but also according to a pretty intricate numbering system. One of my chores when I was growing up was to make sure the videotapes were in numerical order with those number stickers that came with the blank tapes. So thanks, Mom, for giving me a head start on what would turn into a very serious labeling obsession.

I think of getting organized after the chaos of winter as a wellness activity. Put on some good music, make your favorite tea or pour a glass of wine, and start conquering the messes in your house, your car, your garage, your closet—the sky's the limit here, people. You can even pick a specific day or weekend to do your yearly organizing, turning it into a spring tradition that helps strip away the clutter of the previous year. Maybe it's always the first Saturday in April, and you prep for it as you would any holiday: snacks; a playlist; maybe you have a cute pair of overalls you wear for the occasion. You don't have to send out invitations or lay out crudités, but making it feel festive and special can help alleviate some of the dread most of us feel when it comes to cleaning.

Get the Kids Involved

Another great tactic when it comes to cleaning house is enlisting your kids to help. For one thing, it's free labor (just kidding!), and for another, it teaches them valuable lessons about giving to others and not getting too attached to material possessions. Once they're old enough, I ask my kids to go through their toys and clothes and pick out the things they either don't want or don't fit into anymore or that they would like to donate to a child who needs them. It helps the process move faster (well, sometimes—have you ever tried to "clean" with a three-year old?), and it teaches them to share.

I like to bring them into it because there is always that important moment down the line when they say, "Wait: where is my yellow dollhouse?" That's my cue to say, "Remember we went through your toys together and you wanted to give it to a little kid who doesn't have a dollhouse?" It's always nice to help them remember and understand. I never get rid of a toy that they aren't ready to part with because I'm sentimental and believe we all have our reasons for keeping things. But at the same time, yes—sometimes I do nudge them if it's something I think just needs to go, like shoes that are too small or the Buzz Lightyear doll they don't play with anymore because they're into Woody and Jessie. If it's a favorite of mine that reminds me of their happy baby days, I put it aside and store it in a bin of their keepsakes.

Throw a Party

If you cannot bear the thought of cleaning and organizing alone (or even with your kids), then turning it into an event is a great way to create a yearly tradition that you'll actually *want* to keep. You can have a clothing swap party, a decor swap party (trading a candleholder for a small vase, for example), a baby-gear swap, or all of the above. Invite your friends, set out some drinks and food, put on your favorite playlist, and ask your guests to bring the clothes or gear they want to trade. There are no rules—it's just a fun event that helps you purge the stuff you don't need and maybe even score a few things you do.

That said, if I've just finished spring cleaning and I don't want to bring a bunch of new stuff into the house, I sometimes just set up these swap parties for my friends. It's a great excuse to hang out, and they can take whatever they want from my "pile." It's so nice to see my kids' things get a second life. When I'm scrolling through Instagram and see my friends' kids wearing the shoes, clothes, or accessories I gave them, I get so tickled. It really is sweet. Then it's up to my friends to decide what they want to donate afterward, and I don't have to second-guess my choice to get rid of something, since I see it getting a good home.

Declutter as a Couple

Believe it or not, Nick and I have turned spring cleaning into an excuse to have some "us time." With three kids and two careers, it's hard to find time when we can be alone together, so we spend a day in the garage or in our bedroom blaring music we love on Pandora and going through things, deciding what stays and what goes. We'll usually put on a Rolling Stones, Led Zeppelin, or Journey station if we're out in the garage and something like a Halsey or P.M. Dawn station if we're in the bedroom (which is a little sexier). We make it fun, trying on clothes and getting each other's opinion about a dress or a suit or an old T-shirt. The process brings up so many great memories. It's a good way to make spring cleaning less tedious and to persuade your significant other to help you out. It's definitely nice to have the manual-labor help. I feel like we move more quickly when we work together, and I always make sure Daddy has his Miller Lite so he's happy while I'm barking orders.

Box It Up

Although I love purging things, spring cleaning is also the perfect time to make what I call sentimental boxes. I was inspired by *Fixer Upper*'s Joanna Gaines, who shared photos on Instagram of keepsake boxes she made for her kids. I have one box for each child, and little by little I put things in them for the kids to treasure (or toss!) when they're older. I'm sure I'll have to edit the boxes one day, but until then, they're filling up with special pieces—the outfits they wore in their newborn photo shoots; their hospital

caps, swaddles, and bracelets. Maybe I'll add a pair of shoes they loved or a book they couldn't get enough of. For now, I'm filling their boxes with sentimental things until each of them turns five. After that age I feel like the material things aren't as sentimental, and I'm more focused on the young people they are turning into. Plus, who wants to sort through eighteen years of boxes?! Not me. I'm just saving things that transport me back to those special moments when they were little. I can pass the boxes down to them while sharing stories about each item and giving my children a little piece of their history. It's also helpful to have your kids create their own keepsake boxes as transition places for items they're attached to but are growing out of. Brooklyn has a ton of "friends" (aka stuffed animals). There are so many she doesn't play with or need anymore, but she's not ready to get rid of them just yet, and I can understand that. So I created a section in the attic with a box of toys she doesn't want now but doesn't want to get rid of. We say it will go to her kids one day, and that puts the biggest smile on her face, which in turn puts an even bigger smile on mine.

Give Back

We always think of the winter holidays as the time of giving back, but what about the rest of the year? The tradition of purging your old things each spring can also become a yearly ritual of giving back to your community. There are so many amazing organizations that will take clothing or shoes or electronics to help the needy. If I know that my clothes are going to single mothers who need professional outfits for their job interviews, then I'm more inclined to part with something I may have been on the fence about. I know it's going to a woman who truly needs it.

The "out with the old" concept isn't just about making room in your closet for more; it's fulfilling on an emotional level as well, and I think that's a spring tradition worth perpetuating. Also, so many young moms need all kinds of baby gear. I give old, extra, or unused suitcases and duffel bags to organizations that help foster children. Foster kids are continually relocating, and they often use trash bags to move. It breaks my heart. There is so much we can do to pay it forward and help make the future bright for someone else.

Reward Yourself

As a last resort, if you're still saying, "I despise cleaning and organizing so much that I refuse to even look at a label maker," you can give yourself a reward if you go through with the job of cleaning house. It can be a massage, a new purse, or a fancy pair of yoga pants you'd normally not buy out of guilt. Whatever gets you up and motivated and inspires you to tackle that old pile of shoes in your closet is fine by me. You worked hard, right? Reward yourself, especially if it's the only thing that'll get you to do some spring cleaning. When you purge things, you make room for new things, so treat yourself and fill those empty spaces (but not too much!).

Vanessa's Spring Cleaning Tool Kit

Nothing will make you lose steam faster than setting out to get your house in order but not having the right equipment and organizational tools to make it happen. Be sure to gather your supplies *before* the day of your spring cleaning session so you have no reason to put it off for another day (or year). Not only will it make everything easier, you'll also be more likely to *stay* organized and not slip back into the habit of making piles, piles everywhere. Plus, there is just something so soothing about opening a cabinet and seeing everything labeled and put in its place.

LABEL MAKER: I use these for *everything* (yes, I have several of them). I actually get excited when it's time to pull a label maker out. You don't have to worry about bad handwriting, which is a huge plus for some of us! I swear, Nick writes like a seven-year-old boy who's using the wrong hand and hurrying because he has to go to the bathroom. He's someone who could definitely use a label maker. Once you start using them, you will never go back. You can get a compact one or a larger one and even pick the color tape you like. Clear and white are my go-to colors. For the kids I love ordering personalized colorful, washable labels. The thing I learned (after the fact) is to use their first *and* last names. Who knew there would be so many kids with the name Phoenix? But there's only one Phoenix Lachey, and boy, is he cute!

PLASTIC BINS WITH LIDS: I have these in several sizes, and I use them to store the things I don't use every day, like seasonal items (sweaters and swimsuits) and holiday decor. That way you don't end up frantically searching through drawers and closets for your summer things, hidden under a pile of winter coats. I make detailed labels (like "Christmas: Kitchen" or "Easter: Table-scape Decor") so it's easy to find what you need each season.

METAL OR PLASTIC LABEL HOLDERS: I put these on organizing baskets so I know what's inside. It sounds like a huge pain, but it only takes a few minutes, and it'll save you a lot of time and stress later on. Use these for things you handle every day, like the open baskets in your pantry that hold snacks for the kids. I just label them according to which snacks are in which basket so I don't have to rummage around. Pro tip: I wouldn't suggest using one of those tiny dry-erase labels, since the kids can easily smudge them when they reach in to grab a snack. Just print (hello, label maker!) or write the label by hand and change it when needed. I put the baskets low in the pantry so the kids can be independent and learn the alphabet. When the kids say, "Mom, can I have a snack, please?" I always say, "Of course you can. You know where the snacks are. You can grab one yourself. Thank you for asking so nicely." Usually it's followed by huffing and puffing. Sometimes I get lucky with just an eye roll, but trust me, if the kids are hungry enough, they'll go grab their snack, and I pat myself on the back for teaching them self-sufficiency.

DRAWER DIVIDERS: These create sections within a drawer so you can maximize the space. I use them to separate things like undergarments, socks, and workout clothes. They're so simple, but they can really make a huge difference when it comes to organizing your space. My friend Amy is a closet organizer and stylist. She introduced me to dividers as an even more effective way to organize. For example, I have my socks in a drawer with two dividers, so there are three long sections. On the left side are dress socks; the middle section holds thick socks; on the right side are athletic ankle socks. I absolutely *love* getting socks out of my drawer now. It's not a chore to find another pair of the same kind. Who knew socking could be so much fun?

COMPARTMENT INSERTS FOR DRAWERS: These are different from drawer dividers: think of them as the boxes you have in your kitchen drawers for knives, forks, and spoons. They come in so many varieties. They're really helpful in the kitchen and bathroom, because they keep all your things from becoming a jumbled mess. You can put one in the bathroom drawer and use it to keep your toothpaste, floss, deodorant, hair brushes, and hair ties all separated. Everything has a place, and it makes getting ready much less stressful, since you're not rummaging around in a drawer full of brushes and hair ties and makeup. The best way to start your day is definitely with ease. Using these also helps you discover that you have four ladles or one too many mascara tubes, so you can get rid of excess.

CHAPTER 2

No Heirlooms? No Problem!

I have very few things from my childhood besides my tattered blond Cabbage Patch doll. I did once find a box that held my hospital bracelet from when I was born as well as my old pacifier, but that's about it. So with my husband and kids, I am trying to create a sense of tradition by acquiring heirlooms that start with me and Nick and will then go to our children and, one day, our children's children.

The definition of an heirloom is changing, and gone are the days when you'd want to inherit your great-grandmother's gigantic ornamental armoire or your grandfather's—well, grandfather clock. Younger generations are thinking about heirlooms in a different way, although antique earrings and vintage cuff links are always meaningful. If you're lucky enough to inherit a unique table or cool piece of furniture that you can repurpose, then more power to you. These are our links to the past and a way for us to keep the spirit of family alive. Since I don't really have anything from my family or my childhood to pass on to my kids (unless one of them really wants to display my old Cabbage Patch doll in a hutch or something), turning every-day objects into something special and lasting is a way for me to experience the tradition of passing down an heirloom. If you don't have a beautiful old locket to pass down or if you just love the idea of creating your own heirloom (and who doesn't?), following are a few ideas that I hope will give you some inspiration. If you have your own unique DIY heirloom ideas, share them via social, tag me, and include the hashtag #LifeFromScratchBook. I would love to see them!

Brooklyn's Bracelet-to-Be

I vividly remember being eight years old and playing in my mom's room one night while she was out. Looking back, I realize that my mother went out a lot, maybe as a way to forget certain responsibilities. Or maybe it was just because she loved getting dolled up and being with her friends. My mom had me when she was young and still wanting to go out, which in turn made me want to wait before having kids so I could get all those late nights out of my system. Whenever I would miss her, which was a lot, I would sneak into her room and play with her things. I would go through her shoes, her clothing, her makeup, and, of course, her jewelry.

On one of these nights, I discovered a box full of gold jewelry. When I opened it, I felt like Abu, the monkey in *Aladdin*, dazzled by gold. The neck-laces and bracelets and rings were so beautiful; I had never seen anything like them. I must have played with the jewelry for a long time, because I fell asleep on my mom's bed, right next to the open box. My mom was pretty strict, but every now and then she showed glimpses of another side, a side that was nurturing and loving and maybe even a little lenient. So instead of scold-ing me when she found me on the bed with all her jewelry scattered around, she gently woke me up and asked me what I thought of everything. I told her they were the most beautiful things I'd ever seen, and then I asked her if the jewelry was real—as if I even really knew what that meant! She said it was all real and that one day, when I got older, it would all be mine. I mean, talk about a girl's dream.

That thought consumed me for years, and I couldn't wait to inherit my mom's jewelry. Well, that never happened. Looking back, I think my desire was more about having a piece of my mom than it was about having bling. I was eager to have something that reminded me of her, something that gave me an identity. When I was eighteen years old and she came back into my life (for about an hour), I made it a point to ask about that jewelry. She told me it was gone because a man she had dated persuaded her to sell it all. I was devastated.

Years later, when I was pregnant with Brooklyn, I was gently nudging Nick for a "push present." Any excuse to ask your husband for jewelry is a good one, especially when you're telling him it's for the life you're carrying inside

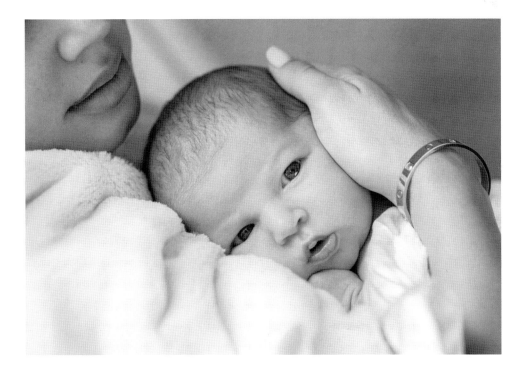

your body. I badly wanted a Cartier Love Bracelet. I knew it was expensive, but I said, "I'm going to have this forever." I love the timeless design and the beautiful way it's meant to be fastened by someone you love. Nick took it to another level as he secured it on my wrist on Christmas Day in 2014. He said, "I'm giving you this with love for our baby girl. Thank you for all you have done and are doing for her and our family. One day, when Brooklyn turns eighteen and she goes off on her own, we will fasten this onto her wrist so she'll always have a piece of us."

I was overcome with emotion, and I launched into a full-on ugly cry. I was nine months pregnant and full of hormones, but still! I often have moments when I know Nick is my person, and that was definitely one of them. I have never taken the bracelet off since that day. Well, I did have to remove it for one Christmas TV movie I starred in because I was playing a struggling law student and it was out of character for her to have a bracelet like that, but that's it. Every other film, TV show, red-carpet appearance—

anything—I've worn it. It represents my daughter, my husband, and my family. It's part of me.

On the day Nick gave me that bracelet, a family heirloom was born, and a new tradition began. Our baby girl will always have a piece of us wherever her life leads her.

The Baby Crib That Keeps on Giving

I've used the same crib for all three of my kids, and as I passed it along to each baby, I realized that they could one day pass it on to their kids. It started with my wanting to spend too much money on our first baby's crib (and room, and clothes, and, well, everything!). So to persuade Nick to cave and be on board with the crib I had fallen in love with, I promised him I would reuse it, since we knew we wanted more kids—and I kept my promise!

You can make small changes to a crib to make it unique for each baby (but be sure to check safety standards, because if a certain number of years have passed you might need to invest in a new mattress). Thanks to my dear friend and design angel, Tiffany, we were able to come up with pieces and unique ideas that were practical and beautiful. I chose a cream-colored crib, and I was able to change the bedding and mobile and accessories to make the room look completely different for each baby. I got a white leather rocker and painted the side table differently for each kid. With each passing day, the crib holds new precious memories that you can share with your kids when you pass it down: the first night sleeping alone, the first attempt to climb out (yikes!), and the moment you knew it was time for a "big-kid bed." The stories and the memories are what make it an heirloom, and if a crib is too cumbersome to keep, you could do this with a rocking chair, changing table, or even a little step stool.

Just for Dad

There are so many lovely ways to create heirlooms for dads, brothers, and sons. My dad was in the military, and I was used to seeing his dog tags around his neck when I was growing up. It was identification for people in the military, and as technology has advanced, dog tags have become essentially symbolic but are still just as important. So one year I got the idea to create a dog-tag necklace for Nick that he could wear always.

When you ask either of us what is the most important thing in our lives and what we are most proud of, we will tell you it's our family. Our kids are the true personification of our love, our commitment, and, one day, our legacy. The idea of Nick having the birth dates of his children close to his heart on tags that he wears every day—well, I couldn't wait to give him that gift. Each tag is dedicated to one of our kids, so now when Nick is on tour or traveling, he has a sweet reminder of each child. Since it's customary for soldiers to wear only two dog tags, I gave Nick one for Camden, one for Brooklyn, and an Old English–style letter *P* that hangs on the chain for Phoenix.

The necklace actually got lost once, and I ended up frantically searching through garbage cans outside on the street—gross, I know, but I did not want to lose that necklace! Nick was leaving for another city, and he was in a panic because he couldn't find them. He usually puts them on the bathroom counter when he's home, and this time they slid into the trash and eventually wound up in a big bin outside. I literally went dumpster diving as I saw the garbage truck coming up our street. Amazingly, I found the necklace, so our DIY heirloom was saved. It's funny how these things can take on so much meaning. That's what these pieces are about for me. It's not about sparkly jewels or fancy furniture. It's about the memories and love within a family and passing those on from generation to generation in unique ways, starting with you.

Storybook Recipes

If you love to cook, creating a recipe box full of personal or family recipes is a great way to hand down old traditions and create new ones. I love getting inspiration from other food lovers, and my friend told me that she made her daughter-in-law a beautiful box containing all her son's favorite recipes—the ones he's loved ever since he's been eating his mom's home-cooked meals.

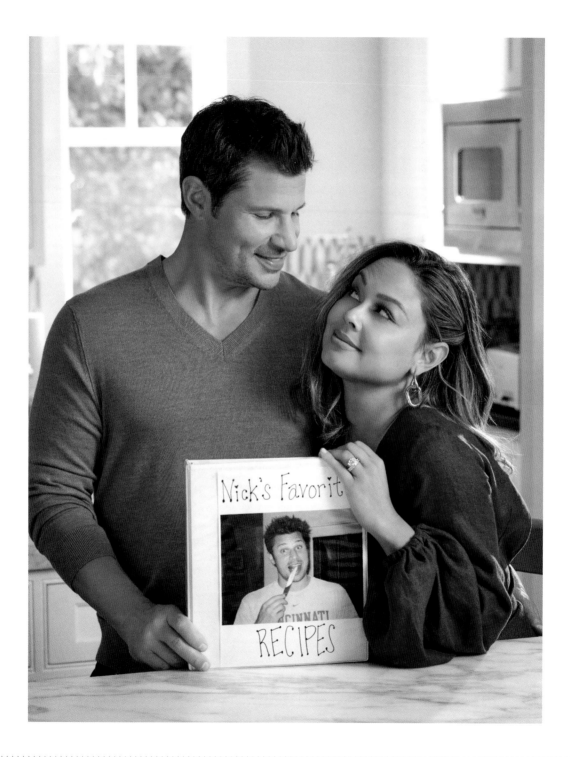

Over the years, I have been given recipes by friends, by Nick's family, and by people I've worked with on shows, especially *Top Chef Junior*, so I fell in love with the idea of making my own recipe box and adding favorites like my Lachey Lasagna (page 206), which is also a perfect home-cooked dish to take to new neighbors, new moms, or old friends who need a treat.

The recipe for a home-cooked specialty is a beautiful gift. You can write the recipes on cards and put them in a pretty box or create a folder or book. I guarantee you will be flipping through the pages for years to come. I made a recipe book called *Nick's Favorite Recipes*, which seems to get thicker with each passing year. I started this book when we were newly dating. In the picture he's licking the icing from the first cake I made for him on our first birthday together. Since we have the same birthday, November 9, it was special to me and to us.

To make it extra special, I like to include little handwritten stories with each recipe, to give future generations a piece of family history that they might not remember or have been around for. If your handwriting is terrible, then type them. Also, in this day and age, we can print anything from the internet and stick it in a binder, so taking the extra care to write and assemble the book yourself makes it a special heirloom. Maybe your son always loved your triple-layered brownie squares and there's a funny story about the first time he tried it, or your daughter accidentally spilled too much of a spice into a marinade you were making and made it even better—those are the little moments that get lost if no one writes them down. Adding stories to each recipe is a fun way to keep traditions and memories alive.

CHAPTER 3

Easter for All Ages

So many Easter traditions are geared toward kids, from dyeing eggs to getting colorful baskets of candy and toys to meeting the bunny himself to the grand finale: the epic Easter egg hunt. Nick and I love entertaining, and we saw an opportunity to get everyone involved so the parents don't have to just stand around and watch the kids. Over the years we've turned Easter into a yearly tradition that's just as much fun for the adults as it is for the little ones.

Every Easter Sunday, we have friends and family over to the house, and we ask everyone to dress up, even just a little. It makes the day feel more special, plus it leads to some great frameable photos. If the kids (and adults) want to kick off their shoes halfway through the day, that's fine! It's not stuffy; it's just an excuse to wear something that commemorates the holiday and makes it feel different from the other 364 days of the year. Plus, some people come from church in their Sunday best!

I spent my first Easter with Nick in Los Angeles, with his family. His brother Drew and his sister-in-law, Lea, were always the host and hostess with the mostest. I loved the way they tag-teamed the day when it came to duties. It makes it so much easier to enjoy yourself. Just having a partner in general makes it more fun to entertain, and so when I am hosting either with Nick or with a friend, I try to make the setup fun, with music and maybe some pre-party drinks. I think if you can look at entertaining as an opportunity to make memories rather than as a chore, you will enjoy yourself more—which is kind of the whole point, right?

Another tradition we learned from Drew and Lea is the adults-only Easter egg hunt. The game has become a springtime tradition that our friends really get into. It seriously turns grown-ass men and women into absolute maniacs, probably because the golden egg has a hundred-dollar bill inside. One guy in particular (G., you know who you are) takes it so seriously that I have to watch him like a hawk every year to make sure he's playing fair and not monopolizing the hunt. I discovered that his tactic was to watch *me* because he knew I knew where the golden egg was hidden, and so when people were close to it I would stand up or look concerned. Damn! He won three years in a row before I caught on to his scheme.

Here's How It Works

Each guest picks a number out of a hat. I get these numbers ready before the guests arrive, so I'm not scrambling to tear up scraps of paper and write numbers on them. This is why the RSVP list is so important. No RSVP, no egg hunt for you!

There are three eggs hidden for each guest, with their corresponding numbers written on each egg. So if you pick the number 1, you have three eggs labeled 1. Early in the morning, Nick hides the eggs. In each set, one egg is easy to find. The next egg is medium-tough to find, and the last egg is a challenge. We do this so when people pick their numbers, one person isn't stuck with impossible-to-find eggs while another person's eggs are in plain sight. When the hunt begins, guests start searching for their three eggs.

Once people have found their three eggs, they have to show them to the host, and they can then search for the golden egg, which has one hundred dollars inside. You cannot claim the golden egg until we see your three numbered eggs first. I made this rule one year after a guy found the golden egg first (hey, it's an imperfect system), so we had to hide it again. We find eggs all year long from people who gave up on finding their three eggs, so I've learned to never, ever put chocolate in the eggs (it melts). Jelly beans and hard candy or stickers and tattoos are a much safer bet.

We also have an Easter egg hunt for the kids, of course. No hundred-dollar bills, though. The Easter bunny (always Nick in costume) hides the eggs around the yard while the kids wait inside. Then they run out and collect them. I admit I love watching my husband dressed in a giant bunny costume throwing eggs around the yard. It's a tradition I cherish. He gets to be a kid again. It's something that's sweet to see, and I don't take it for granted.

For the Easter party, I make a few traditional Easter dishes like deviled eggs (Nick loves these), a few different flavors of mac and cheese, and a ham. With three kids, I am a honey-baked ham girl. I would rather spend my Easter having fun instead of glazing a ham every fifteen to thirty minutes. No, thanks!

Easter Bunny Fails

Make your Easter bunny appearance quick, and make sure to have a talk with your partner about what age your kids are going to be when you tell them that it's Dad or Mom dressed up as the bunny. One year Nick hung out in costume a little too long, and Camden's friends became convinced

it was Nick because they could see his neck through the back of the costume. Epic fail. Then the next year, Brooklyn was screaming because she was scared to see an almost six-foot Easter bunny. I had to calm her before she passed out from hyperventilating. I took the costume's head off and showed her that underneath, it was her dad. Let me tell you, *that* didn't go over well, either. Later that year she found the costume in the attic, and I reminded her that he dressed up for our party as the Easter bunny. But I also assured her that the *real* Easter bunny still came in the morning with baskets! He was cute and tiny and furry and fast as lightning. No one ever saw him. That Easter she sat next to Daddy-dressed-as-bunny with a scowl on her face. She made it very clear she was not a fan of Daddy bunny, even if it was only a costume. You win some, you lose some.

If you don't have the time to make food for everyone, turning the party into a potluck is always a good option. I used to feel pressured to make everything, but I've learned that my friends want to help out, and they take pride in their dishes, too. It's always good to make a specific spreadsheet or list of items so you don't end up with five plates of deviled eggs or all desserts and no veggies or sides. I basically send out an email like the one below so people can sign their names next to the dishes they want to bring.

HAM: Vanessa

MAC AND CHEESE: Vanessa (2 kinds)

VEGGIES/SIDES:

SALADS:

APPETIZERS: Vanessa (charcuterie board and deviled eggs)

FINGER FOODS:

DESSERTS:

ROLLS:

Rolls are always a good choice for a friend who doesn't cook or who is short on time. Of course, people are allowed to add fun and surprising dishes of their own. A potluck is a great way to test a recipe, too. If it's good, you can take all the credit and revel in your success. If no one touches it, you can just slowly walk away as if you have no idea who made it.

Easter Cocktail Ideas

MIMOSA STATION: **I love throwing parties, but I also love *enjoying* the party, so I try to make things as simple as I can. Creating drink stations frees you from having to spend all your time behind the bar mixing cocktails, and since our Easter parties take place during the day, I set up a DIY Champagne-**

and-cocktail station so people can make drinks whenever they want. You can put a few bottles of Champagne in a pretty ice bucket surrounded by orange juice, peach juice, Aperol, and/or sparkling water. I like to add a platter of fresh strawberries, blueberries, raspberries, and orange slices. It looks pretty and is super low maintenance. Just make sure you have plenty of chilled Champagne on hand.

SPIKED ICED TEA STATION: You can also put out a large pitcher of plain and/or flavored iced tea (peach and hibiscus are springlike and delicious) and let people add their own rum. Or you can mix in the rum yourself right in the pitcher. Include colorful garnishes such as lemon and orange slices, mint sprigs, and berries.

SPIKED LEMONADE STATION: I have Nick make the lemonade in the morning, and I put it in a serving jug with a spout. Yes, he just uses a mix, but when we run out during the party I can say, lovingly, "Hey, babe, can you make some more lemonade, please?" Anything to make it easier for me while I'm juggling the food. I add sliced lemons to make it look pretty. Then I set up a table with a few vodka bottles; nice glassware, including nonbreakable options; plus lemon slices, ice, and a stirrer.

BUNNY MOCKTAILS: It's easy to throw together a festive drink for the kids on Easter. Mix colorful juices like cranberry and orange juice with some sparkling water, grenadine, maraschino cherries, and an Easter-themed garnish for a Shirley Temple–esque drink that's not too sugary but looks pretty in pictures. Or if your kids are like Camden and drink only water or milk, fun cups can make it festive and personal. I like giving the kids their own cups, and I always give them their drink stations—with easy kid snacks, too, so they feel like the grown-ups.

MENU

SPICY TUNA
avocado, milo cones, wasabi tobiko

HOUSE MADE RICOTTA TOAST
cherries, pistachio, sunflower honey

OVEN ROASTED TOMATO TART
cornmeal crust, herbed goat cheese,
lemon thyme, aged balsamic

CHAPTER 4

Springtime = "Me Time"

Every spring, I have what I like to call a "mini emotional breakdown." After the holidays, I find myself exhausted, stressed, and depleted. It's hard to transition to the upbeat energy of springtime when all I want to do is crawl under a weighted blanket and sleep for a month. One time I went to see my doctor to try to figure out what was going on with me every spring and why I felt like I was operating on fumes at the same time each year. I asked her to check my thyroid (it was fine). Then I asked about my emotional state. Was I depressed? Why was I so tired and crying all the time? My doctor looked at me and simply said, "You're a working mom of three, and the holidays just passed—you're stressed and burned out." I think her words gave me permission to take a step back and take care of myself.

Ever since then, spring has become my season of self-care. Many parents (moms especially) lack "me time," so why not start a spring spa-day tradition that helps you recharge? Or a "springtime is me time" challenge, when you spend a month doing things that make *you* feel Zen? I know many people have started a tradition of "self-care Sundays," which sounds like a great idea to me! Find a system that works for you, and stick to it. Maybe you can spend a few hours every Sunday reading a novel. Or maybe you start journaling or take a class in something you love but never have time for, like cooking or art or ceramics. Maybe you want to take sound-bath classes or go on a silent retreat. There is no "right" way to do it. Wellness and "me time" are personal, so figure out what works for you and treat yourself.

For me, it's a massage, a haircut and color, getting my nails done, and having a long lunch with my best friend, Jennifer. I know looks aren't everything, but let's face it—when we know we look good, we feel good. A fresh cut and color can do wonders. The massage helps me focus for a bit on what my intentions are and what I want to accomplish. Lunch with my BFF provides the sounding board I need. I vent, laugh, cry, and brainstorm with her. Then I feel like I'm ready to embrace spring and burst out of my winter funk. Do I want to start a workout class? Are new recipes on the horizon? Or hey—maybe I'll write a book! I don't do all these in one weekend, of course. I spread them out, but I make sure to get them in as best as I can.

Having a supportive partner or friend or family member who can wrangle the kids during your "me time" is crucial. It's not really "me time" if you're giving yourself a pedicure while simultaneously making school lunches and folding laundry. Don't cheat yourself!

Yes, it's only a week or a day or even an hour, but this tradition allows you to check in with yourself and see how you're feeling about your direction in the new season and new year. Take the time to figure out which little rituals help you recon-

nect with yourself, then see if you can blend those rituals into your everyday routine throughout the year in some small way. Maybe you discover that five minutes of meditation every morning changes your entire outlook and lessens anxiety, so you can try to work that into your routine. And with all the new apps available, we can really be accountable. Sometimes we need an extra nudge to get us started and keep us going. For example, Nick and I downloaded the Calm app. It offers meditations and affirmations and helps us connect. Partners can talk about the morning message or the positive affirmation and check in with each other in a meaningful way. I also started a new morning tradition of writing for five minutes to start my day—before coffee, brushing my teeth, or saying good morning to the kids. I do this in waves, but especially when I need the extra love. I freewrite about what I am most grateful for. It's a beautiful thing when you are in a funk.

You can't be everything to everyone and fill their cups if *your* pitcher isn't full, so springtime is the perfect season to indulge in this much-needed "me time" and fill yourself up. Make it a tradition—one that's created by you just for you.

CHAPTER 5

Spring Fiesta

Throwing a springtime fiesta (aka a Cinco de Mayo party) has become one of my favorite entertaining traditions. Maybe it's the gorgeous vibrant colors, the delicious food, or (most likely) the margaritas and palomas, but I tend to go all out when May 5 rolls around.

Going all out doesn't have to be stressful, though. You just need the right music, some colorful plates and decor (think reds, yellows, and oranges for napkins, plates, and cups), a simple taco station—maybe with some enchiladas, guacamole, seven-layer dip, and chips—and you're good. Our kids love this tradition now, too (minus the cocktails, of course), and it's a great excuse for them to have their friends over so they can play and the adults can . . . play, too! Not to mention eat.

Fun fact: a Taco Tuesday dinner was the first meal we had together as a family of five. What I mean is that instead of the kids eating dinner at 5:00 p.m.—and by "dinner," I mean buttered pasta and fruit—and then the adults eating steak and potatoes at 8:00 p.m., after the kids had gone to bed, we had a 6:30 p.m. dinner of tacos, guacamole with all the fixin's, and rice, all *together*! At the same time! As many parents know, this is a near miracle, and whenever I think of spring and Cinco de Mayo, I think of that bonding time and our first meal as a full family. Taco Tuesday is what really kick-started our Cinco de Mayo tradition, and it's something that has become special for our family. I hope we're still enjoying it when the kids are grown and they can bring *their* kids.

Now that the kids are a little older, it's definitely easier to get everyone to sit down and eat together, but that doesn't make this tradition any less special. Taco Tuesday is our special night whenever we want, throughout the year. I added some things to our fiesta night to make it work for large groups, including an enchilada casserole and more dips and appetizers. This spring tradition doesn't have to happen on May 5, either, but it's a beautiful holiday that's about amazing food, great drinks, and celebrating the season—paloma in hand, of course.

CHAPTER 6

Mother's Day

For me, Mother's Day is a time of reflection. I like to take a beat and appreciate the family I have and think about things I'm proud of, or things I can work on. It's kind of an extension of the self-care I mentioned above, but I've found that establishing a pattern of "taking care of me" allows me to stay in tune with myself and not get overwhelmed by the madness that is motherhood.

To commemorate the occasion, I started a tradition of secretly sending emails to an account that Nick and I created for each child, and reading the emails I've written throughout the years on Mother's Day. The kids can open and read all the emails when they turn eighteen, but right now they have no idea that the notes exist, which I find really sweet. Nobody has time to scrapbook anymore (unless you are an OG craft master, in which case *I envy you*), so this kind of tradition is an easy and meaningful way to create something special for your kids.

We all have phones full of photos and videos of our partners and friends and kids (especially our kids), so sometimes I'll include a video or photo along with a quick story about it so it doesn't get lost over the years.

Some of my favorite emails are about special moments the kids experienced over the course of the year, like the day Camden hit all his baskets in his basketball game and was beaming with pride. I added a video capturing that moment to accompany the sappy proud-mom email. I wrote in detail about his self-discipline that whole week as he shot baskets in the driveway and how proud Nick and I were. Below is one of the first emails I wrote, when Camden was almost a year old. This is the email that kicked off the entire tradition, and then Brooklyn and Phoenix started getting emails when I was pregnant with them.

July 25, 2013

Hello, my sweet boy! It is 8:00 p.m. on Thursday, July 25, 2013. I have been wanting to start an email account for you since before you were born. Your dad and I LOVE you so much and have so much we want you to always remember, cherish, and have forever! This is the best way for us to keep everything in one place. We will keep up with it over the years and add to it as often as we can, and then when you graduate from high school and head off into the world in whatever way you wish to, we will share this special account we created for you WITH you! You are our beautiful son. Our light, our love, our everything! We feel like the luckiest parents in the world to get a boy with such a sweet disposition. We have said that since the day you were born! As I am writing this, you are asleep in your room, and I just came back from the gym because I start filming my new Fox TV show called *Dads* on August 14, and I need to be in hot mama shape! Ha-ha! I gained sixty-five pounds with you, boy! And I feel like it was all belly. ;-). Dad is away on tour—"The Package" tour with Boyz II Men, 98 Degrees (his group), and New Kids on the Block. His tour ends August 5, but he is home EVERY chance he can be to spend time with us! He LOVES YOU SOOOOO MUCH I feel like he could burst at times. It was really sweet last night when Daddy was here (he had two days off) and he sang you to sleep. He sang "Sleepy Eyes,"

one of the songs on your lullaby album, and you kissed him without his even asking for it. It definitely was a sweet and special moment, and Daddy was so happy and proud. You know, he wrote that song for you! He came up with the melody when I was pregnant with you, and he would hum it almost every night. Then, once you were born, he put words to the music . . . and that's how "Sleepy Eyes" came about.

We love you, and we can't wait for the adventure you are about to give us!!! Definitely our favorite part of life so far!

Love always and forever,
Mom

I'm sharing this personal email with you before Camden sees it because I hope it inspires you to start an email account for your own little ones. You can send an email as quickly as you can pick up your phone—or you can even write it one-handed while feeding them. You can talk about anything—a child's first big-kid bed, how he felt about it, and what that first night was like for you as he kept crawling out of it (fun times). You can write about your daughter's first day of school, accompanied by a photo. Or her first ride on Daddy's shoulders and what it meant to him. Moving forward, I can imagine emails about the time Camden got his driver's license and drove out of the driveway by himself, or the first time Brooklyn fell in love and got her heart broken. But the bottom line is that life happens, and things pass us by. It's nice to capture it. Try it out for a year, then go back and read what you wrote. Include how you felt during the moments you're writing about, because once your kids are parents (or we're old and can't remember things), this will be an amazing tradition they can pass on and a beautiful way for them to experience your memories of their growing up.

For several years, I've had to travel for work on Mother's Day. I hate being away from my kids. (But I'm not going to lie—being alone on a five-hour flight and then staying in a hotel all by myself can be a pretty fantastic gift.) So despite the fact that we're not always in the same place, Nick started another Mother's Day tradition that has grown with our family. It began when Camden, our first, was born. That year, Nick gave me a framed photo of him as a baby. Each year the photo evolves, so when Brooklyn came along the photo was the two of them, one holding a sign that said HAPPY and the other holding one that said MOTHER'S DAY. When Phoenix was born, they each held a sign, and one year Camden actually handwrote his (be still, my heart!), and so every year I know the photo will hold some special surprise as the kids continue to grow and change.

Mother's Day holds a different meaning for everyone. Maybe you love taking your mom to afternoon tea every year, or you like to just sit in a nice bubble bath all alone and *relax* while your partner entertains the kids all day. For some people, it's a holiday that brings up complex emotions, because they're either missing a mom or maybe they don't have a great relationship with her. Whenever these feelings have come up for me, I find solace when I remember that the tough emotions are what made me stronger and made me a better person and mom.

It's a personal holiday, and I would love to hear your unique Mother's Day traditions. You can share them with the hashtag #LifeFromScratchBook to help start a conversation about what the holiday means to people across the globe—and maybe even inspire a few new traditions along the way.

CHAPTER 7

Springtime Gardens

There is something so satisfying about gardening. Even when my kids come home from school with a bean planted in a plastic cup, we're all buzzing with anticipation when a leaf sprouts and we watch their little plants grow. Then starts the arduous job of keeping the thing alive so the kids don't think you're a failure—or, worse, that *they're* a failure!

The year 2020, as most everyone can attest, was incredibly challenging for many reasons. For some of us, it ignited a creative spark, either as a way to maintain sanity, to keep the kids occupied, or just to cure boredom. For me, a lasting memory from the coronavirus pandemic will be the fear of going to the grocery store, then afterward, spending an hour sanitizing myself, the groceries, and the fruit and herbs I'd just bought. Since I was trying to minimize shopping trips, I would buy way too much, and our produce would go to waste (except for all the bananas, which benefited from the cultural phenomenon known as the banana bread comeback).

When I was working on *Top Chef Junior*, I was amazed by the farm-to-table concept, and in my heart I wanted to be a farm girl (even though I live in the heart of Los Angeles). Once we were all quarantined at home, I realized it was the perfect time to live out my farm-girl fantasy, and the gardening began. I also figured it was something we could do as a family so we wouldn't kill one another out of sheer boredom.

We started by simply growing herbs by the kitchen window. Let me tell you, when you're making bruschetta and you need fresh herbs, walking over and cutting some out of a pot on your windowsill is much more satisfying than buying them at the store. There are so many amazing herbs you can grow, but I think for beginners the following make a great start.

PARSLEY

BASIL

ROSEMARY

CHIVES

MINT

You could try cilantro or dill or fennel or oregano, but I like the five above because I cook with them so often—basil for Italian dishes, parsley and rosemary for hearty soups and roasts, chives for mashed potatoes and egg-salad sandwiches, and mint for some weekend mojitos. Just pull some fresh mint leaves out of *your own* garden, muddle them with lime juice, add sugar, rum, and some club soda, then pour it all over ice. Garnish with fresh mint, and *bam*, you're a professional mojito-drinking farm girl.

Once you have mastered the simple herb garden (by the way, there are tons of starter kits online and in stores), you're ready to move on to fruits and vegetables. You can get your partner involved and truly make it a family affair. It's also extremely therapeutic and relaxing. My kids love helping pick the veggies and fruits when they're ready to harvest, and it's a great way to teach them responsibility and follow-through.

Vanessa's Gardening Tips

Gardening can be therapeutic, but it can also be stressful until you get the hang of it. Here are a few tips I learned along the way that might help.

1. LOCATION, LOCATION, LOCATION: **Don't just plop a garden down anywhere. Most veggies need at least six hours of sun daily, and you don't want too much wind or a lot of foot traffic. Make sure the plot is easy for you to get to and maneuver around. You don't want to stomp on your kale while you're trying to pick your tomatoes.**

2. MAKE A FRAME: **Create a moist and well-drained space. If you don't have one, you can easily make a frame with some rocks and wood. This is the most strenuous step, but it's necessary for a successful garden.**

3. PLANT WHAT YOU EAT: **If you *hate* squash, that's probably not the vegetable for you. Also think about perennials (which return each year) versus annuals (which need to be replanted each year). Most veggies are annuals. My favorites are bell peppers, cucumbers, garlic, and tomatoes. My favorite fruits are raspberries and strawberries.**

4. ORDER: **When all else fails, there are tons of starter kits for those of us with no green thumbs, or pinkies, or index fingers. These kits are a great way to get started and get you motivated in the kitchen. Plus, some have cute planters. Make it fun! Not a chore.**

PART 2

Summer

Summer is all about freedom, sunshine, and finding creative ways to entertain your kids. It's the perfect season to start some traditions that will help fill the days and nights with memories, whether they involve wrangling young kids, relaxing with friends, or spending some quality time with your partner.

Summertime makes me think of lemon cake, melting popsicles, road trips, travel, sunshine, beaches, backyard dinners, and later bedtimes for the kids (a blessing and a curse). One summer we lost power (twice) because it was so ridiculously hot in LA, and we had to improvise to keep the kids entertained. We lit candles at night, blared music from the car stereo through the open kitchen window so we could have impromptu dance parties, ordered pizza, and played cards and board games—which, miraculously, held the kids' attention, since there was nothing else to do.

It's crazy how much we depend on technology. I'm the first to admit that, *yes*, I have an iPad for the kids when we're on a plane or if I have a deadline to meet and need to finish some work or, heck, if I need one or two or three of them to stay occupied so I can make dinner. Technology can be a lifesaver, but it's also nice to be reminded of the good old days of outdoor playtime, and gadget-free fun. I mean, with no power I couldn't charge the electronics, so it was back to basics—getting outside and enjoying the fresh air, sunshine, and occasional mosquito bite.

I remember riding my bike to friends' houses on my own at a young age. Yes, I was riding my bike at six years old with no parent in sight! This sounds crazy to me today. Once, I ran my bike into the back of a parked car. I knocked out my five front teeth. Well, I picked three of my teeth up off the concrete and rode home holding my teeth and crying, with blood all over my pink T-shirt. I had two more teeth that had to get pulled later that day at the dentist. Maybe this is why I helicopter-parent my kids when they're on bikes and scooters. Still, there was something nice about the pretechnology days—if you don't count the (five) missing teeth.

As a kid, I loved building forts, playing hide-and-seek, and even playing in the car while my dad was in the garage fiddling around. So do my kids, which is sweet. I'm not gonna lie, though—it's tough to put away the tech and entertain your kids for hours on end, but whenever I do, I *never* regret it. I will say, Nick is a huge help with the outdoor nudge. He loves being outside, and his excitement is contagious.

Summer is the perfect time to take a step back, unplug, and create traditions that help make the season special, whether your power is out or it's business as usual. It's about lazy days and warm nights. Firecrackers and birthday cakes. Swimming-pool splashes and BBQ on the grill. And, yeah, the occasional Instagram post to capture those memories.

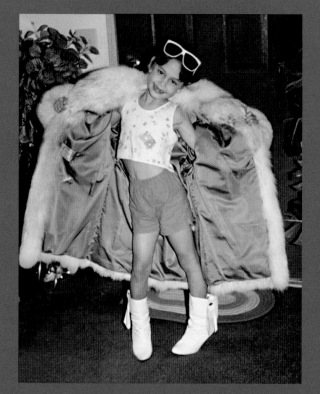

Little Vanessa with no five front teeth.

CHAPTER 8

A Logo for Every Birthday

Summertime gets me looking forward to outdoor birthday parties—balloons, bounce houses, the works. Camden is the only one of our kids with a summertime birthday, and when he was little I started a yearly tradition of creating a unique logo for each of his birthdays, something that could easily be printed on shirts, hats, napkins, stickers, the cake—you name it. If you want to do this, too, you can go big or keep it simple, whichever works best for you. Maybe you're thinking, "Why would I spend time making a logo for a kid?" I get it. But if you want to add some personal touches to a birthday, this is a pretty cool way to do it. Plus, it elevates your party with minimal cost. You can print the logo on stickers and slap them on dollar-store bags and cups to make them look festive and "custom." I do this for Halloween, Easter, and summer BBQs, too. If there's a party, I'm there with the logo stickers!

The first thing I do when I'm making a logo is to come up with a theme—with the kids' input, of course. That is, unless they're babies, in which case, it's Mama's choice. Soon enough they start to get opinionated, and if you've ever dealt with a headstrong toddler, you know that "opinionated" is an understatement.

Over the years we've had themes for Camden's birthday like Lachey Racing (since Camden was into cars), Camden's Minions (*Despicable Me* was his favorite movie that year), Camden's Construction Site (baby Camden was all about the construction trucks), Super Camden (this incorporated all super-heroes), and Lachey Ninja Warrior Family, for which we created an *American Ninja Warrior*–type obstacle course, including a warped wall like the one they have on the show. The emcee of the show, Akbar Gbaja-Biamila, came to the party as a surprise (one of the perks of being in the TV business), and all the kids' shirts said AMERICAN NINJA WARRIOR.

At the party, we'll all wear matching hats or shirts with the logo on them. This makes for a great photo op, because it's one of the rare times I make it a priority to get all five of us in a picture. Usually it's a sweet photo, but some years there's at least one screaming child in the mix. C'est la vie. My mom was big on dressing us in matching outfits during my childhood birthdays, so maybe in a way I'm carrying on that tradition. You don't have to be a graphic design whiz or an artist to create a fun, meaningful logo, although having a friend who's a graphic designer doesn't hurt—shout-out to my friend Heather at River & Bridge. It also doesn't have to be expensive. It's a fun way to make each birthday memorable, and the matching hats, outfits, and decor make for great photos and keepsakes.

Below are a few tips I've learned over the years that will give you some logo inspiration for your next summer birthday party, whether for adults or kids.

- It's always fun to incorporate the guest of honor's birth year or initials in a cute way, like adding EST. 2012 to a logo or, if you're doing a truck theme, adding something like TRUCKING SINCE 1980. With your adult friends,

you might want to check with them to see if they want their birth year displayed all over the place for everyone to see before you design your logo. I had fun with Nick's fortieth birthday, when I wrote NL EST. 1973. Now I can use those shirts and logos at every party I ever have for Nick. You better believe I will be pulling

them out for his fiftieth, fifty-fifth, and sixtieth—you get the picture. For kids, stamp that sucker on everything from the napkins to the party hats. Ah, to be young and carefree! Camden knows that his *C* logo is special and unique to him, so it's a fun treat each year when he sees his birthday cake (and hat and stickers and shirt!).

- To print stickers, buy sheets of them (just as you would buy sheets of labels for your label maker) and print them at home. (Heather usually prints them for me.)

- You can also create a unique "family crest" as your logo. This is great because it can last for years and you can get super creative. Incorporate fun elements like your daughter's favorite color or your son's favorite animal. The sky's the limit with this idea.

- I also asked Heather to design a Lachey font, which I love, and now it's on my Christmas cards, thank-you cards, envelopes, and gift tags. I order everything in bulk (which saves money and time) and can use them whenever I want throughout the year. You can either design your own font or just choose one and use it on everything. I love the recognition it creates, turning something as simple as lettering into a tradition that people come to expect. I chose a color called "gold foil" because it's always in season.

- Plan ahead! This may sound obvious, but creating a birthday logo requires some time, so don't attempt to design and print your logo the day before the party or you might wind up frustrated. This is meant to be fun. To make it easy, start designing a month or so ahead, so you don't feel rushed and can enjoy the process. I'm not saying you need to work on this night and day for a month, but giving yourself some time makes it a stress-free tradition you can look forward to each year. Once it's finished, everything else is easy and can be done at the last minute—if you like living on the edge. Whatever else happens, the personalized logo gives it that "I've been planning this for months" feel, even if you threw it all together in a frenzy! For example, we once had a menu change on the day of a party, but I just printed the menu out again on my home printer and put a new logo sticker on it. No one knew the difference.

SCRATCH THAT

Logo Mistakes

Proofreading is so important! The last thing you want is 150 stickers that say HAPPY BIRTDAY or THIS IS YOU'RE YEAR! How embarrassing! Have a grammar-conscious relative or friend read over what you've written just to make sure you haven't misspelled anything.

Another trick is to read the text backward, from the end to the beginning (the sentences, not the actual words). This way you can more easily see spelling errors. It's weird, I know, but if you try it, you'll see what I mean.

Finally, ask one more person to look it over! Three is a good number of proofreaders. If your logos get past all three readers and there is *still* an error you missed, then you can have a drink and laugh about it at the party—plus, you can all blame one another!

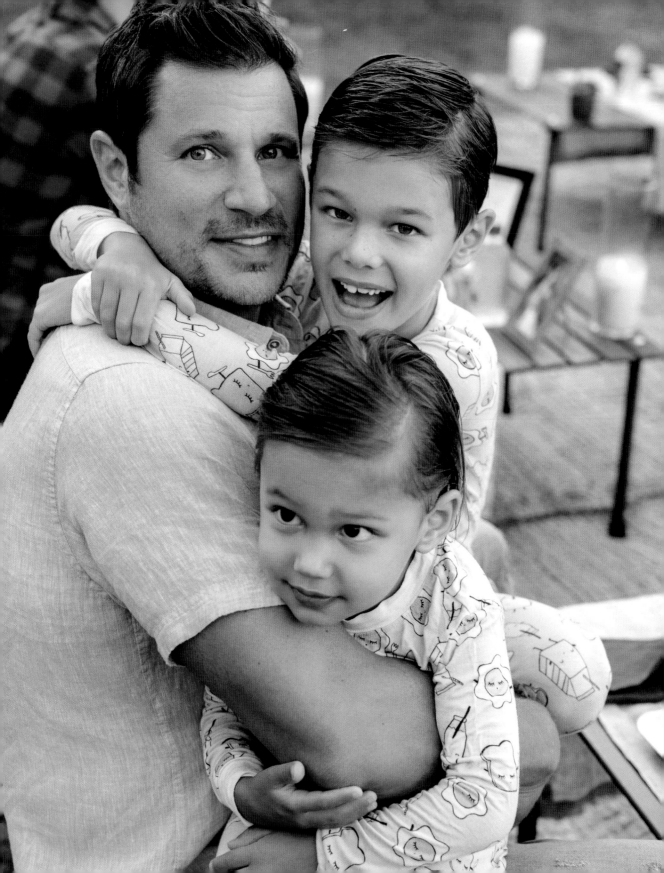

CHAPTER 9

A Little "Me Time" for Father's Day

Over the years, we developed a tradition of giving Nick some "me time" on Father's Day. Basically, he goes off with his friends for a few hours and just does what he wants—which, to be honest, usually involves sports and beer. That away time is good for the soul—and for our marriage. The tradition started after I had worked four Mother's Days in a row, which meant I had plenty of "me time" relaxing in a hotel room, ordering room service, and watching whatever I wanted, like every Melissa McCarthy, Tina Fey, or Tiffany Haddish movie ever made. Since it was such an amazing indulgence, I decided to do the same for Nick.

We are very hands-on parents, and we love being with our kids (although sometimes Mom and Dad need a break), so it's nice to create a tradition that lets us regroup and have some alone time. Plus, when your partner comes back from his "me time," he's motivated to help *you* by taking out the trash, doing the dishes, or maybe even rubbing your feet and saying thank you for the "me time" earlier in the day. It's a win-win scenario.

Father's Day isn't all about Nick being on his own, though. Once he's had his guy time, we'll then celebrate that evening as a family, with a dinner or special gifts from the kids. (We've learned to not try for Father's Day breakfast, because Nick is an early riser, but I, on the other hand, will lie in bed and pretend to sleep as I smell bacon frying in the kitchen on *my* day if it means breakfast in bed!) It's easy to get overwhelmed by our day-to-day responsibilities and forget to give holidays like this a little extra significance, so whether it's a homemade card or a favorite dessert, following are some simple ways to create meaningful Father's Day memories.

Father's Day Craft Ideas for Kids

PAINTED DAD'S DAY HAMMER: This is a fun object that's easy to create. Just buy a basic wooden-handled hammer at your local hardware store and let your kids decorate the handle with paint or markers, making Dad a personalized tool that'll always remind him of the little ones. You can write the date or a special message on the handle and turn an everyday object into something sweet. The hammer Camden made sits in Nick's office, and just by looking at it he's filled with memories of that special day.

FINGERPRINT BASEBALLS: This is an adorable gift that Dad can keep on a desk or dresser. Just buy a few baseballs or softballs and have the kids dip their cute little fingers in paint and press their prints on the ball. You can write a personal note with the date and turn that year's Father's Day into a memory he can cherish for years to come.

"DAD LIBS" CARDS: Instead of the traditional Mad Libs (a game in which you supply words to fill in the blanks, resulting in a funny or nonsensical story), you can make Dad Libs cards with the kids. Just get out paper, glue, scissors, and decorations so they can make an imaginative original card. Inside the card you can glue a template (just google "Mad Libs Father's Day templates") that prompts kids to fill in the blanks in sentences like "My dad is a _____" and "He always helps me _____." It's a sweet, funny surprise that will definitely put a smile on Dad's face.

PERSONALIZED TIES: It's fun to surprise dads not with a regular old tie but with a *personalized* tie. One year, Nick got a hilarious tie that had our dog Wookie's face printed all over it. You're probably thinking, "Sounds funny, but I bet he'll never wear it." *Au contraire!* He will wear that thing to daddy-

---

SCRATCH THAT

Color Fails

Maybe let your little ones use all the colors of the rainbow on their personalized hammers—except red. The year Camden painted his hammer bright red, the thing looked like a lethal weapon. After that, Mommy learned to use happier colors, like blue or green or yellow. Just a suggestion!

daughter dances and father-son events with pride. Once he even brought it out when he was cohosting *Live! with Kelly* during their Father's Day special. The tie was the talk of the show that day. You could also make custom socks to match the tie, and on the card you could write something like "We're tied together forever," because who doesn't love a good dad joke?

CHAPTER 10

How to Up Your Summer BBQ Game (Even If You're Not Great at the Grill)

My husband is what I'd call a nervous griller. He's always worried that the chicken will be too dry or the burgers will be too raw—or, on the flip side, that they'll be burned because he was overcompensating. He once got so close to the grill that he lost part of his eyebrows and a section of hair, down to the scalp. We called him Uncle Bic after that (he used a Bic lighter to relight the grill, and his brother Drew is quick with the jokes).

Summer Party Tips

- I always place extra towels out by the pool, because inevitably someone will forget a towel or two. This way no one needs to run into your house dripping wet! If you want to make sure your towels don't go missing, write your name on the tag with a Sharpie. It may sound silly, but with three kids, we label everything they own for school and camp, so if someone sees a towel that says LACHEY at their house, they can return it.

- Leave out buckets of ice with bottled water, plus some extra sunscreen for guests. If you aren't into the plastic, just set up some sort of station for hydration. A jug with flavored water always elevates things. Or set out lemonade and juice boxes. Again, nothing fancy, just a place where people can hydrate. The last thing you want is for a guest to get heatstroke—talk about ruining the party!

- If you don't have a pool, you can set up sprinkler games or a Slip 'N Slide course. You could also have a water balloon party, which is a nightmare to clean up afterward, but it's a blast for the kids. You could also set up a "bike course" with cones so the kids can ride their bikes or scooters around the obstacles. Or maybe you could host an ice-cream-sundae party or a sidewalk-chalk party.

- I like to put out a bunch of toys for the kids, so they can just grab what they want without having to ask you to go inside every five seconds to get a new toy to play with. They'll probably still ask, but at least this way you can point them in the direction of the toy pile. Throw in some goggles and dive toys to keep them occupied for a while.

- If you're having a pool party, hire a lifeguard! This has helped tremendously when we have people over to swim. I know what you're thinking: "I'm not paying to have someone watch my kids while we have a casual backyard BBQ!" Let me tell you, *this* is my most valuable tip. If you don't want to spend a lot of money, then hire only one lifeguard. Enlist a kid from the local youth center or a college kid who wants some extra cash (but make sure he or she is a certified lifeguard, of course). If you want to get fancy, hire two lifeguards, and they can play games and actually swim with the kids. Lifeguard babysitting! It's around twenty-five to fifty dollars an hour, and if you pay for two or three hours, it helps the parents relax a little bit, knowing that someone is keeping an eye on the little ones. If you ask me, you can't put a price on pool safety. At one party we had, there were kids jumping off the rocks into the pool, and the lifeguard asked the kids to stop, and I didn't have to be the bad guy *or* go to the emergency room for stitches!

Vanessa's Summer BBQ Playlist

The best way to set the mood for your summer BBQ is to create a great playlist, and I could share hundreds of songs I love, but following are just a few to get the party going.

"Gypsy" by Fleetwood Mac
"Carry On Wayward Son" by Kansas
"More Than a Feeling" by Boston
"Don't You (Forget About Me)" by Simple Minds
"Any Way You Want It" by Journey
"Dream On" by Aerosmith
"Keep On Loving You" by REO Speedwagon
"Love Is a Battlefield" by Pat Benatar
"Sweet Home Alabama" by Lynyrd Skynyrd
"Take Me Home Tonight" by Eddie Money
"Livin' on a Prayer" by Bon Jovi
"Lyin' Eyes" by the Eagles

Since he had a bald patch right before he shot the live finale of a show he was filming, he had to have a patch of hair made, like a tiny toupee, to cover the spot, which was applied by special-effects experts. So yeah, he's a nervous griller, and he burned his own hair off. That doesn't stop us, though!

When it comes to summer BBQs, we've created some traditions that even the most unskilled cooks (love you, honey!) can handle. We're not trying to outgrill Bobby Flay; we're just trying to have some fun. But tell that to Nick.

For our summer parties, we'll have the traditional BBQ fare (burgers and hot dogs), but we make it unique by adding personal touches that people can remember and look forward to.

Over the years, my lobster rolls have become "famous" among a small group of Nick's friends who come to our backyard BBQs, so in addition to Nick's grilling skills, the lobster rolls have become part of the yearly rotation.

Tradition is all about the small personal touches you bring to a moment or an event to make it special, and summer BBQs are a great way to create a tradition for friends, family, and kids. When you send out an email or a text inviting people to your yearly BBQ, it's fun to have their first thought be "I can't wait for those Lachey Lobster Rolls and Minnillo Beans" or "I hope Nick breaks out the cornhole." Nick is a cornhole master. In the summer months, he loves to play in his swimsuit with a beer in hand—for balance, of course!

CHAPTER 11

The Friendship Exchange

I would not be able to stay sane and juggle motherhood, work, and marriage (and everything in between, like visits to the pediatrician, baseball practice, soccer games, after-school enrichment, dance class, endless school events—you get the idea) without a close group of female friends. These relationships are like a lifeline. They offer support, love, humor, gossip, and the occasional—and much needed—bitch session. Who else can help you navigate topics like marriage, the lice outbreak in the third-grade classroom, coordinating basketball and soccer games, where to get facials and waxing, and ways to survive toddler meltdowns?

Here's a great example of leaning on friends. One night, Brooklyn was being wild, and she fell and hit her head on the floor so hard that I heard it from two rooms away. In a panic, I reached out to the moms on my "Soccer Moms" text group, asking what I should do. (Was her brain okay?! Should we rush to the ER??) One of the moms was a pediatric ER nurse, and she eased my worries and helped calm my stress (thank you, Brenda!). At times like these, having your girls to help out can save your sanity.

Since International Friendship Day is July 30, and National Friendship Day is the first Sunday in August (so you can celebrate twice!), summer is the perfect time to honor the women (and men) in your life who ground you, support you, and keep you laughing.

One year, my friends and I created a gift-giving tradition that allows us to show how much we appreciate each other. It also helps us save money and time, since we don't feel pressured to think of a wildly creative or extravagant gift for every single girl on every single birthday. The older you get, the harder it is to plan a girls' night out or a weekend away with friends. In fact, it's nearly impossible. Implementing simple traditions in the name of friendship is a great way to keep in touch and strengthen those bonds without trying

Communicate!

Before you agree to go in on gifts together, have an honest and open discussion about expectations. We all have a friend who's like, "Let's go big!" And another friend who's thinking, "I have three kids and bills to pay, and I'm a stay-at-home mom; I'm not down with *big*." If you don't communicate, things can get if not ugly, then uncomfortable. Just be honest and loving. Set a price limit. Throw out numbers. Is it twenty-five dollars per person? Is it fifty dollars per person? Is it one hundred dollars per person? Keep in mind, you do this for *all* the girls in the group, and you will also get a fabulous gift! My friends and I had an honest talk, and we all agreed on contributing fifty dollars per person. There are six of us, which leads to a nice gift! It also lets you budget that money for the whole year on gifts for your core group of BFFs.

to coordinate a major event or pick the perfect birthday gift year after year. But . . . if and when you do go on a girls' night out or a trip away . . . *go!*

The night we came up with our "friendship gift" concept, we were at a restaurant in LA called Gwen (owned by my *Top Chef Junior* cohost, Curtis Stone). When our meals came, the waitstaff offered us a tray of steak knives, each one unique, and said, "You may choose whichever one you want for your meal." I loved the personal touch and the idea that we all had steak knives but they were all different. In some ways it symbolized our friendship—we were all different, had different tastes and personalities, but we were bonded by our friendship and love for one another.

That year, one of the women in our group wanted a small rose gold heart necklace for her birthday. It was dainty, perfect, and cute—and when we split the cost five ways, it was, like, forty-five bucks each. Individually, we would have spent that on a candle, a gift card, or some home-decor item she doesn't need. So we all pooled together and got it for her. We loved it so much that we decided that we would each get this necklace in a different color—like the knives, the necklace colors showed our different styles and personalities— and a tradition was born. (Fun fact: I got yellow gold and it's the necklace I'm wearing on the cover of this book!) Since then, every year we've all gotten matching jewelry for one another. The following year it was a bracelet, after that a ring, and it's still going strong.

I cherish my "mommy tribe." These women were there for me when I was in the NICU with Phoenix. During that time, they created meal trains for Nick and Camden and Brooklyn, ran errands for us, and lent overall emotional support. Then during quarantine in 2020, I evolved my school mommies into my "Quaran-Team." They step up when life gets tough, and they're always there for a laugh or a cry. It's so worth it to take the time to honor these friendships, whether it's your mommy tribe or your college friends or your small circle of BFFs. Having everyone chip in on one gift a year makes it a communal tradition that lets them know how much you care. Every time I wear a piece of jewelry from "mah girls," as we call one another, I think of our bond, and it makes me smile. It really is a beautiful tradition and a reminder of our friendship.

I have my core girls, but as life evolves, so do new friendships. When the coronavirus pandemic of 2020 hit, these bonds are what got me through. We asked one another questions, sent funny memes, shared articles, requested "drive-by" birthdays or hellos for the little ones, and scheduled happy-hour Zoom "meetings." At the end of the day, no matter how strong, smart, in control, and boss lady you are, you need an outlet and a shoulder to lean on. You need a safety net and friends to tell you they got your back. Friendships take work, something I learned relatively late in life. I wish I knew it earlier, but being a military brat, I was never in one place longer than a year or so,

Girls'-Night-In Playlist

Spending quality time with female friends is a must for me. It rejuvenates me; it allows me to let go and unwind and have some fun without my husband and kids. If I have some friends over for wine, food, and bonding, there are a few songs I like to have on hand to keep the energy going.

"Let's Hear It for the Boy" by Deniece Williams
"True Blue" by Madonna
"1999" by Prince
"I Can't Wait" by Nu Shooz
"I Wanna Dance with Somebody" by Whitney Houston
"Straight Up" by Paula Abdul
"Everything She Wants" by Wham!
"Bust a Move" by Young MC
"Into the Groove" by Madonna
"Tell It to My Heart" by Taylor Dayne
"Push It" by Salt-N-Pepa
"Girls Just Want to Have Fun" by Cyndi Lauper
"It Takes Two" by Rob Base and DJ E-Z Rock
"I Think We're Alone Now" by Tiffany
"Shoop" by Salt-N-Pepa
"Any Man of Mine" by Shania Twain

until high school. Now I know that the work you put in you get back. Love your friends; respect them; nurture them. Friendship is a beautiful relationship that needs lots of TLC.

CHAPTER 12

The Summer Giveback

As a teenager, I did volunteer work every single summer. Not gonna lie: my parents made me do it—but I am so grateful they did. I started out at the VA hospital when I was fifteen years old. My dad and stepmom were both in the air force, so helping war vets meant a lot to my dad. I know he was trying to keep me busy and out of trouble during the summer months, but I was also learning valuable lessons. I learned responsibility, because people depended on me. I also learned empathy. You truly don't know what it's like to walk in other people's shoes until you have spent time with them and heard their stories. I have so much respect for all our veterans and active military. I try as much as I can to support them and never forget.

When I got older, I started volunteering at the children's hospital in Charleston, South Carolina, which was both rewarding and heartbreaking. It solidified in my heart how badly I wanted to be a mom. I would get so excited to see the kids' faces light up when they had visitors or received gifts or just heard a joke that cheered them up. Seeing their smiles was amazing, but the experience was also extremely hard—seeing them go through things as children that you could never imagine going through as an adult. It puts life into perspective.

My point in telling you this is to remind you that we all have our own struggles. It's important for me to instill some empathy and the desire to give back into my kids' hearts, and it's something I will always continue to do. We all are connected in some way, and it's our responsibility to raise good humans. Summer volunteering, whether it's in a hospital or at a shelter or with an environmental group, is an amazing tradition to start for you and your loved ones.

Still, I vividly remember huffing and puffing at my dad for "making" me volunteer during the summers, when everyone else was on Jet Skis and traveling to faraway beaches or amusement parks. I was so jealous. We didn't have that kind of money growing up. We were fine, but my dad and stepmom both worked, and summertime didn't change that. What I didn't realize at the time was that these summer volunteering experiences would change my life and become a tradition that I would strive to pass on to my kids.

Camden's elementary school has a motto: "Keep kind in mind." It's one of the reasons I fell in love with the school. Even at six years old, he started understanding kindness and empathy. So I try to remind him gently, as often as I can, how important it is to take the time to do good things for other people. After all, the children are our future, as Whitney Houston sang!

Fun fact: my mom used to make me karaoke that song when I was five years old for *all* her dinner parties. She had me dress up in a full "look"— poufy dress, lace ruffle socks and nice shiny shoes, hair done, and karaoke mike in hand. Then she'd say, in her thick Filipino accent, *"Banessa, sing da song . . . the chilren song!"*

I had forgotten how embarrassing it was until I watched a Jo Koy stand-up comedy special. Like me, he has a Filipino mom and a military dad, and his childhood "party trick" was dancing to Michael Jackson. I guess it's a thing. Even though I can't sing to save my life, my mom was always so proud. Filipinos *love* to entertain, and they have dreams of their children becoming

Volunteering Checklist

When it comes to volunteering, there are a few pitfalls to avoid if you want to make the experience positive for everyone.

- First, triple-check and make sure you're volunteering for or donating to a legitimate organization. Ask friends if they've ever volunteered with that organization so you have some references, and check with watchdog groups like Charity Navigator and CharityWatch. The Better Business Bureau also has a Wise Giving Alliance, which rates charities.

- Make volunteering fun for the kids, not a chore. If you're bagging items to donate, for example, put on music, set some snacks out, and turn it into a fun activity, even if it only lasts thirty minutes. The kids can be your helpers by putting stickers on things (TOYS or CLOTHES SIZE 7 BOY) so you know what's in each bag.

- Be realistic about time requirements, especially if kids are involved. Make sure you're thinking about short-term versus long-term commitments. For example, Nick was part of Big Brothers Big Sisters of America. He was dedicated and involved for almost ten years, until his "little brother" turned eighteen, and Nick has made it clear that he's still only a phone call away. We've heard stories over the years of people volunteering and then just disappearing, leaving the kids stranded. If that kind of commitment isn't realistic, that's okay—just try to find something manageable for you and your family, like a food drive or volunteering in a hospital for the summer. Anything you can do helps.

famous. I guess when I look at my life now, as an actress and a dedicated volunteer, I realize that my parents really gave me a foundation for performing—and giving back. Basically, that's a long way of saying, start 'em early.

PART 3

Fall

Fall is by far my favorite season. It's the smell of cookies baking, warm vanilla candles, peppery stews, and steaming mugs of tea (or a hot toddy). It's all about cozy sweaters, warm blankets, and fuzzy socks. What's not to love?

Fall is also about going back to school, which when I was a kid meant riding in my stepmom's Datsun 280Z, sometimes *in the trunk* because there was no room to sit anywhere else. Don't worry—it was a hatchback, so I was basically lying down in the back with the AC on, and I could hear the radio. My brother and I would make her stop a few blocks before school so no one would see us climbing out of the hatchback. Thank goodness there was no social media back then, because a few times some kids from school spotted us, and we'd be mortified for the rest of the day. But that would be it. There were no Facebook posts or Instagram pics to prolong our embarrassment. Ah, the good old analog days, when phones had a cord and screenshots didn't exist.

Maybe I try to make back-to-school traditions fun and positive for my kids because of those old, traumatic(ish) Datsun 280Z memories. Moving schools so much as an "air force brat" made this time of year a little tough for me. So I like to ease the transition by doing things that get my kids feeling hopeful and help calm their nerves as a new school year begins.

There are many other things to celebrate during the fall months, from Halloween to Thanksgiving to Sunday football, so get your pumpkin-spice *everything* out, and prepare to indulge in some fall traditions that will make your year just a little bit cozier.

CHAPTER 13

The Back-to-School Dress Rehearsal

Now that Nick and I have three kids, we've perfected the whole back-to-school thing so that it doesn't feel chaotic or stressful in the least.

Just kidding!

What we *have* done is develop a tradition that (we think) helps ease the transition from long summer days to early alarm clocks, bus stops, and new teachers. Since the change to school days can be tough, I try to make it as fun as possible. Think confetti, balloons, and a special breakfast. I'm not making gourmet pancakes in the shape of Elsa or anything like that, but I try to make it festive so the kids can wake up feeling enthusiastic instead of overwhelmed and grouchy.

Since we noticed that our oldest, Camden, was often tired or out of sorts on the first morning of school (who wouldn't be?!), Nick and I started a tradition of doing a "dress rehearsal"—a run-through of the first day of school—the day *before* the first day, so that the kids (and parents) can go through the motions of early wake-ups, getting ready, and getting to the bus stop on time. Leave it to parents who work in entertainment to create a dress-rehearsal tradition for their kids, but it works! It helps them ease in so they're not jolted by the new routine on the *real* first day of school. Plus, they're usually sleepy on the actual night before school since they woke up so early that day. It's a win for Mom and Dad!

Sample Back-to-School Dress Rehearsal

Here's how it goes down.

- We still lay out the uniform. Because it is pants or shorts and long sleeves or short sleeves. Our school has a few different color tops. Bottom line, lay out what you are wearing so it's all ready.

- At bedtime, we let them know that Daddy's going to come into their rooms at 7 a.m. and that they will be leaving for school at 7:50 a.m. This way we set an expectation, and maybe one day it will sink in and they can get themselves ready on their own. LOL! Sorry—just a moment of parental delusion . . .

- At 7 a.m., Nick goes into each kid's room, starting with Camden and ending with Phoenix, singing to them and getting them out of bed. Camden, being my firstborn, gets dressed first thing! The other two need time to wake up. Every kid is different, right? So we go potty and head downstairs to eat breakfast.

- Once they're done with breakfast at 7:30, we head back upstairs to brush their teeth, then get Brooklyn and Phoenix dressed. We brush their teeth first because toothpaste dribble on their school uniform can be catastrophic to a kid. Plus, then we'd be late cleaning up or changing. Live and learn. Once everyone is dressed, we do their hair and go back downstairs to head to school.

- At 7:45, they grab a backpack and water bottle, and head to the car. At 7:50, Nick is pulling out of the driveway. This is Nick's favorite time of day with the kids. He talks to them and sings the whole way, when they let him. You'd think the kids would be all about Dad's voice, but it's still embarrassing when it's *your* dad.

- On dress rehearsal day, they obviously don't go to school, so at 7:50, they go get pancakes. A pancake tradition makes back-to-school something they can look forward to. Yes, they already ate breakfast on back-to-school day, but kids always seem to have room for fresh pancakes. Plus, Daddy is always there to finish their breakfasts . . . how convenient.

CHAPTER 14

Going All Out for Halloween

There is an entire side of our garage devoted to Halloween costumes and decorations—and it's a pretty big garage. What can I say? I love Halloween.

Halloween for the Grown-Ups

Nick and I threw our first Halloween party the second year we were together. He hadn't proposed yet, so I "slyly" suggested that we dress up as Bride of Frankenstein and Frankenstein (*hint, hint*). I went way over the top and wore a wedding dress I found at Goodwill. That first year when we threw a party it felt like we were creating something unique and lasting, just the two of us. Now we've been throwing them for more than thirteen years, with no plans to stop. I hope we still have the energy to dress up in costume when we're in our seventies, even if the costume is just a unicorn onesie and some house shoes.

When I start planning our annual party, I first brainstorm a theme with my trusty sidekick and friend Corrie. We have the same twisted-fun party mind! Maybe it's a boneyard, a carnival gone bad ("carnEVIL"), or old Hollywood ghosts. From there, everything falls into place, including the costumes, the decor, the cocktails, and the food. Of course, you don't have to have a theme to throw a Halloween party, but I think it makes each year memorable and fun for the guests, since it inspires them to get creative instead of relying on a witch hat or a vampire mask year after year.

One year we set a house-of-horror theme, and I hired people to dress as iconic scary movie characters: Michael Myers from *Halloween* was at the entrance (but also protecting the entrance), Jason from *Friday the 13th* ran around the party with a (fake) chain saw, the guy from *Saw* was riding his tricycle down the hallway to the bathroom door, and the bartenders were dressed as butchers. As I said, I don't mess around when it comes to Halloween.

Our Halloween party has become such an important tradition in our lives that we try not to schedule work or trips in late October. Talk about dedi-

Halloween Hosting

One year Nick and I threw our party on Halloween weekend (this was before we had kids). I thought it was a great idea, but then *none* of my friends with kids could make it. They said, "Don't you understand how important this day is for the kids?" I didn't at the time. So my suggestion: throw your party the weekend before or even two weekends before Halloween. I promise it's not too early. People love getting dressed up for Halloween, even way before the day. Just make sure to give your friends who aren't Halloween fanatics plenty of notice, so they have time to get a costume together!

cation. Friends even text us a few months in advance to ask what the year's theme is so they can plan accordingly. We never skip it. Even if we have to hold the party two weeks before Halloween because of our schedules, *the Lachey Halloween party is on*. Did I mention that I love this holiday?

If you're hesitant about planning a party because of the time involved, remember that you don't have to make it so complicated that you feel like you're hosting the Met Gala in your living room. You can make it as simple or extravagant as you like. Make the theme a general one, or pick a theme that's easy to create a party around, like "ghosts" or "monsters and margaritas." You can also serve simple appetizers like chips and dips and cheese trays, and have bowls full of different wrapped candy with bags so people can take home an easy favor. Hold a costume contest, put on some great music, and call it a day!

If you want to take it a step further, you can create a whole candy station, make some cute party favors for people to take home, and lay out a delicious Halloween buffet that adds to the ambience and fun of the night. I

like my candy station to have full-size candy bars and empty goodie bags so the guests can stuff the bags themselves and take them home in addition to the party favors. When we had an old Hollywood theme, I made the candy table look like a graveyard, with foam headstone and creepy moss, and it was perfect. You can even put Jell-O shots in plastic syringes on the candy table.

Halloween Hack

I like to save some of our leftover Halloween candy and add it to our Advent calendar. It's fun to surprise kids with something like a Ring Pop in December, and it reminds us of fun memories from Halloween.

Scaring the Kids—but Not Too Much!

When Cam was little, Nick and I had the bright idea to get a six-foot-tall animatronic skeleton that moved and spoke. Well, as you can imagine, it did not go as planned, and Cam was terrified! So we started calling the skeleton Mr. Bones and dancing with it and hugging it to show him that it was fun instead of scary. Ever since then, all our skeletons have been named Mr. Bones, and our kids don't get freaked out. Try to explain that Halloween is funny-scary instead of scary-scary to help them enjoy the holiday.

Halloween for the Kids

It was shocking for me to discover, but Halloween isn't *just* for adults. Now that I'm a mom, I know that having kids makes the holiday so much more memorable and fun. Who can resist the sight of a baby or toddler in a pumpkin or lion costume? Or a little kid dressed as Albert Einstein or an Oompa-Loompa? I live for it.

I love including my kids in the Halloween planning, since the anticipation of holidays and traditions like this is half the fun. A few weeks before October 31, we love to bake fun treats for them to share with their classes at school—anything from a cupcake with intricate icing to a pumpkin-shaped cake (ugh . . . thank you, YouTube Kids, for giving them that idea) to a doughnut decorated with plastic vampire teeth and eyes.

I get the kids involved in *all* the Halloween decorating so they are not scared by it. I string the cobwebs, and I have them put the tiny spiders everywhere. We put out Mr. Bones and dance around with him. I know this may not work for all kids, but Nick and I have found ways to make the scariness of Halloween fun and silly so they can enjoy it, too.

CHAPTER 15

How to Host Thanksgiving and Not Lose Your Sh*t

For most people, hosting Thanksgiving sounds about as relaxing as shopping on Black Friday, but over the years I've picked up some tricks that can help you turn Thanksgiving into a tradition that's memorable *and* stress-free. Well, mostly stress-free. That's what wine is for, right?

Nick and I have been hosting Thanksgiving (or Friendsgiving) for years. No matter where they're from or how far away their families live, our friends in Los Angeles know they can come by in jeans and a cozy sweater, grab a drink, watch football, and spend the holiday surrounded by love and good food.

Whether you're hosting your first Thanksgiving or your tenth, whether you're inviting a small group of family or a boisterous group of friends, I hope these tips will help make the experience as simple and fun as possible.

The Planning

My friends and I start talking about the holiday as early as August, figuring out if we're staying in town and hosting or heading back East to celebrate with family there. Then I start seriously thinking about Thanksgiving prep in early November. It helps to have everything organized so you know exactly where last year's decor and plates are and you're not doing it all the day before.

The Prep

I love getting the kids involved as much as possible in all our family gatherings—especially Thanksgiving. I let the kids set the table. It's a big responsibility, and

It's All About the Prep

I will never forget a Thanksgiving early in my relationship with Nick when I was literally sweating in the kitchen. I was so miserable, giving him as many stink eyes as I could muster because he was laughing and chatting and watching football with our friends. I was thinking, "Why am I doing this to myself? This sucks!" Since then, I've learned to prep *everything* the night before and say yes to friends who want to bring a side dish. I've also forced . . . I mean, leaned on Nick to do certain things to help make it easier on me: I have him deep-fry one of the turkeys, he preps some of the food, and on the big day he's in charge of drinks. No one is Martha Stewart except Martha Stewart, and I bet even she accepts a nice side dish or two from a friend. The point is: accept help!

they love it. I also have Brooklyn write out the place cards, which is fun for the guests to see. A child's handwriting adds a sweet touch.

The Decor

I always opt for rustic decor. Think pampas grass, burgundy florals, and deep greens and oranges. I use the same plates for every holiday, but I change up the napkins and flowers. If you invest in nice dinnerware, there's no need to have more than one set. I do like to rent beautiful chargers and glassware for intimate dinner parties, but for family gatherings I use the everyday china we were gifted from our wedding. It's one of my favorite things that we got together, and as the years go by it becomes even more meaningful.

The Kids

You can seat the little ones at the kids' table, but if you have toddlers running around, it helps to set out Thanksgiving Day activities for them so you can eat in peace, at least for a few minutes. I like to have a few crafting projects available in the living room during my prep time so I don't wind up scrambling to find something that will entertain the kids in the middle of the meal. One of our go-to items is a set of plastic fillable Christmas ornaments that the kids can decorate using pom-pom balls, pipe cleaners, markers, or stickers. Then they write their names on their ornaments, and Mommy or Daddy can write the date. When they leave dinner, they have a keepsake for Christmas. Another thing I love to do every year is cover the kids' table with kraft paper (taped down, of course) and leave crayons and markers on top so they can draw. I originally did this because it's hard to decorate the kids' table, and it kept them all busy at dinner while we enjoyed our conversation. Any little projects like this are great to have on hand so that the kids don't start climb-

ing the walls once their pumpkin-pie high kicks in. Craft stores are a great resource, too. They have so many affordable DIY kits for every holiday. I buy a few and place them in trays and stations around the area so the kids can play and create something fun.

The Turkey

There are many times I have screwed up Thanksgiving dinner. In fact, I think I mess up at least one thing every year, but now I can handle it better, and I've learned to not let it ruin my night. I think *everyone's* biggest screwup is the turkey. Will the bird be ready when we want to eat? Is the meat too dry? Is it undercooked? To alleviate this stress, I started cooking two turkeys. If we have a lot of guests, I roast a medium-size turkey in the oven and deep-fry a small one in a turkey fryer. This gives me a safety net if one of them doesn't turn out well. Also, I've learned to roast the bird early and warm it before we eat so there's no mad dash to get everything ready once the turkey is done. But be careful how you warm. You don't want dry turkey meat.

The turkey also takes up valuable oven space. So by finishing it early, letting it rest, and carving it, then placing it in a warmer or covering it with foil, you're less stressed and rushed and the oven is free for all the fixin's. Plus, when the gravy is nice and hot, the turkey, even if it's at room temperature, is still good. No one needs piping-hot turkey, but everyone *will* want hot potatoes, veggies, gravy, and dressing, so focus on that.

All these things can be cooked the night before and reheated on Thanksgiving Day.

In our house, Thanksgiving veers straight into Christmastime. As soon as the kids are in bed on Thanksgiving Day, Nick and I can be found pouring our first Christmas cocktail (always a White Russian) and pulling

boxes of ornaments and decorations out of the attic. Well, he pulls them out and I watch him put his muscles to work. Then we engage in an all-out day-after-Thanksgiving decorating extravaganza.

It started when we were first dating. It was Thanksgiving of 2007 (we decided to travel on our *first* Thanksgiving together in 2006): we had finished dinner and decided to make some cocktails to help us relax while we cleaned up. My dad only drank about once a year, during the holidays, and he always had a White Russian, so in his honor Nick and I mixed a few of those. The flavor reminded me of the holidays and felt festive. Before we knew it, we were pulling out boxes of Christmas decorations, hanging stockings, and putting up wreaths. We got a little carried away, thanks to the yummy cocktails, but right then a long-standing fall ritual was born. It has become just as important as turkey and mashed potatoes on Thanksgiving—maybe even more important, because it's an "untraditional" tradition, the first one Nick and I started together.

CHAPTER 16

A Little Fall Romance

Nick and I have the same November birthday, and even with our hectic schedules we've made it a tradition to take a birthday trip every year we've been together. Before we had kids, the trip would be a week in Fiji, but now it's more like a night in a hotel down the street from our house. Hey, it's a getaway! You have to keep the tradition alive somehow.

Whether you're going to a tropical island or a bed-and-breakfast down the road, this tradition is a great way to add some romance to your relationship and reconnect—and you don't have to have a fall birthday to do it. You also don't even have to leave the house. Creating a fall romance tradition can mean you write each other a love letter every November or surprise each other with something special on a particular day each year, "just because." I think this starts with making the time for the tradition and ensuring that it happens the first few times. Then you'll realize it's something you look forward to.

Most of us try to celebrate our love during anniversaries, but it's nice to create another, more unexpected, holiday that's about nurturing your relationship. Nick and I try to remind each other that before our crazy family started, we were just two kids in love. Keeping that spark alive is important, and it's not always easy, so creating a tradition that allows both of you to refocus and rekindle the romance is key.

V—
Wow! What a year! There is no one else on planet Earth I could ever do this "Life" thing with but you! I love you so much and can never thank you enough for just being you. You ying to my yang... When I'm down ... you're up! We are lucky I deem and I am so proud of who and what we are building together. Please know that I love you more than ANYTHING in this crazy world! —N

CHAPTER 17

Holiday Cards That Don't Suck!

My holiday card tradition started the year Nick and I got engaged. Back then it was just the two of us plus our dog, Wookie, and the star of the show—my engagement ring. I wanted a fun way to tell our friends and family that we were getting married, since he proposed in early November—just in time for the holidays. This was before the rise of social media, so what better way to do that than with a holiday card?

Since then the tradition has evolved into a celebration of our growing family through pregnancies, newborn babies, and the beautiful chaos of being a family of five. When I was growing up, my family didn't send holiday cards (and we didn't receive many, either, because we moved around so much), so as a kid I always envied the rows of cards on the mantels at my friends' houses. I'm sure it was hard for my parents because most of, if not all, their friends were in the military, and moving is an annual event for military families. But now that he's on Facebook, my dad is like a teenager with all his buddies. They crack me up with their photo uploads and shared memes.

I try to alternate the mood on our holiday cards: one year funny, the next year sweet. In the humorous cards, it's about showing life as it is rather than sending a perfect Instagram vision of well-behaved children who never have spaghetti stains on their clothes, never throw tantrums, and never blink when the photographer says "cheese." (I mean, if your kids never do these things, then congratulations to you!)

Whichever year-end holiday you celebrate, photos are a great way to connect with people you don't see all the time. Sending cards allows you to reevaluate your relationships (licking stamps and envelopes is a huge pain—the recipients better be worth it!) and take a step back and reflect on your year. The tradition of writing letters and sending postcards has all but disappeared in the age of email and texts and Instagram, so taking the extra time to keep this long-standing practice alive is a great way to stay in touch and show someone you care.

If the idea of having a photo session (the photographer could be a professional or your BFF), printing physical cards, and addressing those cards sounds exhausting, there are plenty of digital options for sending a holiday greeting. This probably comes as no surprise, but I like to do it the old-school way, and I see it as a fun fall project that helps me reflect on all that has happened in our family over the previous year.

Vanessa's Holiday Card Hack

Plan early. There is no way around this. By the time you take the photos, print the cards, and cross-check your address list, plus juggle Thanksgiving and holiday prep, you might just get too stressed out and say, "Forget it." Start thinking about your cards in October, especially if you don't want to have to pay rush fees or extra postage. I start thinking about the theme of our cards in August!

One of my favorite cards showed Camden as a one-year-old. It was the first time I embraced the idea of a card being perfectly imperfect. The photo showed little Cam crying on the floor while Nick drank a beer, I held a glass of Champagne, and we were both exasperated. I think images like this sometimes make cards better because they're real and relatable. You can show the messiness of life, and people smile and get it.

You can also get creative and base your card on a famous painting. Maybe you re-create a Norman Rockwell scene or redo the iconic *American Gothic* painting with one of you holding a martini instead of a pitchfork. You could add a written update about the major milestones you and your family marked over the previous year, like births, graduations, moves, and new jobs. The more creative you get, the more your friends will look forward to getting your card, turning it into a tradition that's not just for you but also for them. One of my favorite things to hear is friends saying, "We can't wait to get your Christmas card this year!"

CHAPTER 18

Game Day at the Lacheys'

In our house, fall is about football. Every season, Nick's friends know they can knock on our door on Sundays, get some chili and a beer, and kick back and watch a game or two. I like sports, but my husband *loves* sports, so therefore game day is sacred in our house. It has become a tradition that I look forward to—cozy fall Sundays, good food, and the sounds of the game echoing through the house. Plus, it's a fun way for me to feel connected to my husband's world, hang out with friends, and have some fun.

You don't need to be a type A party planner to pull off a casual game day. All you need are a few simple recipes, some beer, and a good bottle of wine to drink while you're cooking. You also don't have to put out a spread *every* single Sunday, either, which sounds exhausting even to me—and I *love* planning parties. Hosting a few fall game days brings family and friends together for a relaxed gathering during those crisp fall days and nights.

So what does game day look like at our house? For starters, it's all about the food. You can order a pizza and call it a day, but if you're willing to put in just a little extra time, you can make things like V's Game-Day Chili (page 195), Lachey Layer Dip (page 167), Jalapeño Popper Spread (page 188), and of course a good ol' charcuterie board.

In case you have a few guests (including little kids) who are more into the chips and dip than the game, you can set up a few activity stations to give them something to do besides watch football. Below are a few ideas that are hassle-free and always fun.

CORNHOLE: This game is easy to set up on the lawn. It's basically just a wooden board with a hole in it and some small beanbags you toss into the hole, and it's great for both kids and adults—the board also doubles as a jungle gym for energetic toddlers. Football lovers can take a break during halftime, and it's a good way to give people something to bond over besides touchdowns. Remember, no cheating: twenty-seven feet from front edge to front edge!

LADDER TOSS: The kids can have fun with this one, too. You can find a ladder toss set on Amazon or at places like Target, or if you're extremely crafty you can build your own. The rules are simple: just toss two balls tied together with string onto the rung of a short ladder. It's a good distraction when guests need to stretch their legs during the commercial breaks.

BEER PONG: Obviously not for the kids! All you need is a table, some plastic Solo cups, Ping-Pong paddles, and a Ping-Pong ball. Nick and I are in our forties, but we're not too old for a little old-school drinking game. Plus it's kind of a workout, right? My tip: add water to your cups and drink from your own beer on the side. Yup, Mommy over here thinking about germs constantly!

It's all about having a good time and watching the game, so I try to keep the kids entertained (or distracted) and away from the man cave of fanatics. I always leave a ton of snacks out for the kids. I don't add a lot of sweets, though, because handling sugar-addled kids solo while Dad is watching the game never ends well. It's not always necessary or possible, but every now and then, if you have a teenage niece or nephew or a family friend who wants to make some extra cash by watching your kids, I always ask. I'll say, "Hey, want to make a few bucks and keep an eye on the littlest ones?" It's nice to have extra hands to help out. It doesn't cost much and allows you to enjoy the day and be present. How many times have you heard people complain that they didn't get to hang out or see the game because they were cleaning or refreshing drinks and food? A babysitter on a busy game day is a nice stress reliever for the parents—which is a win for everyone.

PART 4

Winter

Winter is magical. But let's be real here—it can also be crazy stressful. It's cold; the kids are on break from school; you have to figure out what gifts to give your in-laws and bosses and what you're going to do for the kids' teachers. It's no wonder we start counting down the days until spring break while it's still freezing outside.

Despite the stress, winter is also a season of warmth and reflection. It's pine-scented candles and chocolate chip cookies baking in the oven. It's twinkling lights and cozy pajamas. It's binge-watching your favorite holiday movies (ours is *Love Actually*) and spending quality time with the people you love. It's eating warm chicken tetrazzini (one of my winter favorites and, coincidentally, the meal I ate before each of my kids' births) and enjoying a cozy cocktail.

I continue a few of the traditions that began during my childhood, but most of our winter traditions were started by Nick and me as a way to remember what matters most in life: connection, closeness, and comfort food—not necessarily in that order! For a natural-born party planner like me, this is a season of small get-togethers and big celebrations. Even if you would rather spend cozy nights at home with the family, I hope these ideas inspire you and help make your season just a little bit more magical and memorable in ways large and small.

CHAPTER 19

'Tis the Season

For me, the most exciting thing about winter is the *anticipation* of the holidays—the decorations, the music, and the planning (yes, even that can be fun). Each holiday season, we'll either throw a winter party of our own or head to a friend's house, but either way we love an excuse to wear an "ugly sweater," exchange white-elephant gifts, and get together with friends. This is far from black tie—unless your sweater has a black tie stitched into it. This is jeans and plastic cups of delicious cocktails, sometimes rimmed with crushed candy canes to make them extra festive.

Maybe your holiday tradition is opening a single gift at midnight on Christmas Eve and the rest on Christmas Day. Maybe you make a special type of potato latke for Hanukkah each year using a recipe passed down from your great-grandparents. I love that we all have special things that make holidays unique, whether it's a yearly cocktail pajama party with your closest friends or a holiday bake-off with the family.

It's amazing to realize that the traditions you start today could be celebrated by your kids or grandkids decades down the road. Legacy isn't just about changing the world in major ways; it's also about making an impact on people's everyday lives, whether that's through a gift-giving tradition, a yearly winter board-game extravaganza, or a holiday breakfast casserole.

Speaking of which, one of my absolute favorite holiday traditions happens to be the Christmas morning casserole that I've been making every year since Nick and I spent our first winter holiday together. No joke: I found this recipe when I was dating Nick and wanted to make something easy but yummy. I mean, after all, as they say, the way to a man's heart is through his stomach. I found a recipe online with some sort of title like Granny's Famous Breakfast Casserole—I remember it was made with bread slices. I'm thinking, *yes*—this will impress him for sure and make him want to marry me! Hey, I was twenty-five, so what can I say? I changed the recipe a little, made it my own, didn't call it Granny's, and here we are.

Each year, Nick and the kids can't wait to have this dish. For us, it means the holidays have officially arrived. It's not like it's a gourmet meal, but it's just

Cooking with Kids

I love getting my kids involved in cooking. Sometimes I ask them to do things that are helpful, like picking the leaves off parsley stems and putting them into a bowl for sauce; other times it's just fun to let them experiment with textures and flavors and get used to cooking their own dishes—until they want you to taste their creations. If you're like me, you don't want to discourage your kids or break their hearts, so you try what they give you. I think Brooklyn would actually shove a spoon down my throat if I said, "Nah—I'm good." Hey, I respect her passion! One day I let her into my spice cabinet because I wanted her to smell and see the various spices. The next thing I know, she's mixed apple juice with chocolate syrup and a whole jar of pepper, some oregano, paprika, and fresh chopped parsley. Then she asked me to taste it. I told her that her daddy was the "official taste tester." Let's just say I keep her out of the spice cabinet now.

so comforting and delicious, and it has come to symbolize family time spent together in the kitchen and at the table, laughing, eating, and just being with one another during a special time of year.

The recipe pretty much stays the same, but each year I'll change little things here and there, like I'll substitute premade crescent rolls or potatoes for biscuits as the bottom layer. We even used frozen hash browns one year when I was crazy busy, and it *still* came out incredible! You can't go wrong with it. My go-to ingredient has become store-bought biscuits, because spending time making homemade biscuits isn't much fun when three kids are tugging at your leg. Plus, Brooklyn loves helping me make this casserole now (Phoenix shows a little interest, but he's barely out of the toddler stage). One of her very important jobs is laying out the premade biscuits (specifically, southern-style biscuits) that I've quartered for her. It's so cute to see the look of excitement on her face as she does it. That, to me, is what traditions are all about—little moments of joy or connection that become indelible memories. I hope she'll still want to do this when she's a teenager, and maybe one day she'll pass the tradition on to her kids, but time will tell!

For kids, the weeks and days leading up to the holiday season are magical. They get excited seeing twinkling lights go up on houses throughout the neighborhood and hearing holiday music playing in stores. Each year, Nick and I try to make the buildup memorable for our kids by doing little things that fire their imaginations and get them into the spirit of the season. Following are a few ideas for building the anticipation that makes the holiday months so special for the little ones.

P.O. Box North Pole

A few weeks before Christmas, we set up a little mailbox marked SANTA: NORTH POLE. Then we tell the kids that they can write letters to Santa and put them in the box for "mailing." It's a clever way to get inside their little heads, but it's also a fun activity for them. They draw pictures, they say hello, and, yes, they ask for some things. We've tried to make it clear that Santa doesn't get them *everything* on their lists, but it's nice to give him ideas. I like that they feel the magic of the season when they do this. They get so excited when they wake up the next day and the letters are gone. Yes, it's *another* task for Mom and Dad, but come on—holiday magic ain't easy! We tell them that the elves take the letters back to Santa. Then I have to find a very good hiding spot so I can refer to the letters when it's time to shop.

When the kids get home from school and see the mailbox, they know it's time to start writing their daily (or weekly—this isn't a homework assignment!) letters to Santa. They can ask for the things they want, tell Santa the

How to Make a Santa Mailbox

- Paint a medium-size Amazon box or shoebox silver or white (or cover it in gray or silver paper). Write "North Pole" on the box with a red Sharpie or paint.

- Cut a small slot in the box so the kids can drop their letters inside.

- If you're ambitious, glue on a little red mailbox flag (available at hardware stores).

- Let the kids decorate the box and add their own touches.

things they've done over the year that they're proud of, or just say hello. If they're toddlers, or if they aren't writing yet, I'll play "secretary" and write the letters they dictate to me. Or they can draw their messages.

I encourage them to make the letters colorful and add stickers to them. It gets their creative juices flowing. After the kids go to bed at night, Nick and I read their letters. Talk about adorable. It helps us figure out ways to surprise the kids come Christmas morning. The letters are also fun treasures to keep and store away so you can share them with your kids when they get older (see chapter 2, about creating your own heirlooms).

Reindeer Snacks

When I was a kid, we would leave out little snacks like cookies and carrots for Santa and his reindeer on Christmas Eve. One year on Christmas morning, like a mini Inspector Clouseau, I actually asked my mom to bite into a carrot so I could compare her bite mark to the reindeer's and make sure it was legit. After careful inspection, I was satisfied that the reindeer had come into the house and nibbled a carrot, so the tradition lived on—at least until I got older and realized that Santa and his reindeer *probably* weren't coming into the house for a snack. Now it's fun to watch our kids experience the same kind of wonder.

We're keeping this tradition alive for our little ones, and part of the anticipation comes from asking the kids to help make the treats for Santa and his reindeer and elves. We use a special plate that says COOKIES FOR SANTA, which I received as a gift for my first Christmas as a mommy. It was from Gerri, mother of my sister-in-law, Lea. The plate has become an important part of the tradition, and I give similar plates to friends who are new parents.

We prep our treats for Santa a few days early so we aren't scrambling the night before. We change it up each year, sometimes making Rice Krispies

Treats with holiday sprinkles for the elves—since, you know, elves like Rice Krispies Treats. Once the kids go to bed, Nick and I make sure to take nibbles of the food (tough job) and leave some crumbs. So far, none of my kids has turned into a detective and asked to compare our bite marks with the ones left by Santa, so we're safe. I'm sure that day will come, though . . .

The More Trees the Merrier

When you have three littles with three different personalities, and one of them happens to have a birthday on Christmas Eve, you get mini kids' trees. We started this when Camden was tiny, and now each kid has a mini tree in his or her room that acts as a cute night-light. I let them decorate the trees, so they reflect their personalities. I think it's a fun way to get them involved in the memories we're creating together as a family.

We also have our main "family tree," and it's full of the ornaments Nick and I have collected separately from our childhoods and our adult lives, plus all the ornaments the kids make in school. It's a hodgepodge of colors and materials, and it symbolizes the love in our family. I started getting Nick an ornament each year when we were dating—I got a tour bus once, since I was on tour with him. One year it was a cell phone, since we talked on the phone constantly. Once it was a beer mug, for obvious reasons. It's tough to keep it up, but we try. When our kids move out of the house one day, they can pick their favorite ornaments from the "family tree" so they can carry on the tradition.

Elf on the Shelf (aka Every Parent's Nightmare)

The energy that goes into keeping up the tradition of Elf on the Shelf—where you hide a toy elf in a different place in the house each night while the kids sleep—truly is every parent's nightmare, but it can also be an amazing bargaining tool if you remind your kids that the elf watches everything they do and reports it to Santa. Basically, you tell them that the elf is always watching, so they better be good before the holidays.

If you forget to move the elf (which we do, often), my suggestion is to make up a list of excuses ahead of time to explain why the elf didn't move so you're not caught like a deer in the headlights in the morning. I also keep the elf pretty high up so the kids can't mess with it. Also, after a glass of wine or two, Mama gets real creative with the scenarios and stories about the elf. Like one year when I put the elf in the freezer with an Elsa doll. Just remember that if you go *too* crazy, you'll have to explain yourself in the morning. There are plenty of tips online about Elf on the Shelf, but ultimately it's just a fun way to keep the spirit of the holiday alive in kids' hearts.

CHAPTER 20

New Year's Eve In

If you have young kids *and* you manage to dress up for New Year's and stay out partying way past midnight—then hats off to you *and* your stamina! But if you're like me, after three kids (hell, even after one), dragging yourself out on New Year's Eve sounds like much less fun than cuddling up on the couch with a cocktail to watch the ball drop on TV. With infants in the house, it was a miracle if we made it past 10:00 p.m.

As the kids get older, it gets a little bit easier to get off the couch. If we're feeling ambitious, we'll go on a family trip over the holiday, but our go-to tradition involves staying in, doing a little early celebration with the kids during the day, then staying up as a couple talking about the previous year and our hopes and goals for the months ahead. But even if you're ordering takeout and wearing pajamas, it's nice to bring a little New Year's glitter and glam into the house, so I try to keep up with traditions, no matter how small, so that we can look back and remember how we celebrated each year.

If you do decide to skip the parties and late-night dinner invitations and stay home, you can still make New Year's Eve *feel* like a party with a few simple touches.

GET DRESSED UP: Just because you're staying in doesn't mean you can't dress up. And by "dress up," I mean you can either put on a nice outfit and jewelry, or you can wear some festive pajamas and throw on some glittery hats. Whichever route you choose, dressing for the occasion makes it feel special. You can order matching T-shirts for the family that have photos printed on them, or maybe they simply say something like LACHEY FAMILY 2021. It's inexpensive and easy to have a local or online T-shirt printing shop whip up a design for you, and it's a nice surprise for the family if you keep it a secret until New Year's Eve.

GET COOKING: Some years you want to order pizza, have some wine, and call it a night, and there's nothing wrong with that (in fact, I love those nights). If you're not up for cooking a big spread, you can brighten the mood with a few festive appetizers or desserts to go with your pizza. My go-to dessert is bourbon balls (for the adults, not the kids). Nick *loves* them, and they've come to signify New Year's in our house. For us, this dessert has become like pumpkin pie on Thanksgiving—a yearly "must" and a dish that makes the holiday complete.

GET THE KIDS INVOLVED: Just because they're not staying up until midnight doesn't mean that the kids don't deserve a memorable New Year's Eve. They love the glittery hats, the shimmery decorations, the noisemakers (maybe they love those a little too much), and the sparklers. One of my favorite traditions is "Noonyear's Eve." Basically, the kids have a little party and do a countdown at 11:59 *a.m.* It's a fun way to give the kids their own celebration—and make sure they're not crying and begging to stay up until midnight.

Unless they're old enough for sleepovers, kids often spend New Year's Eve at home with their parents or a babysitter. So it's nice to give them their own

New Year's Day Traditions

I spent much of my childhood in the South, so I grew up eating black-eyed peas on New Year's Day for good luck. I still make them every year, and it's fun for the kids to take a bite and make a wish for a fun and healthy year ahead. On another note, when Nick and I were engaged, we took a trip to Tuscany, and I learned that in Italy there's a tradition of wearing red underwear on New Year's for good luck. So because I'm part Italian, I partake in this sacred tradition—one pair on New Year's Eve and another on New Year's Day, just for extra luck!

celebration and invite their closest buddies. You can set up a bubble-wrap stomp (just lay out rolls of bubble wrap and let them go to town), stage a colorful balloon drop, or create a simple "ball drop" with a store-bought disco ball and some string. Plus the party wears them out, so they're ready for bedtime when it comes, and you can enjoy your bourbon balls and Champagne on the couch or get dolled up and head out guilt-free!

CHAPTER 21

My Funny Valentine

As a couple, our Valentine's Day tradition is pretty straightforward—Nick and I have dinner together, no matter what. Sometimes we go out, but more often than not we find romance over a home-cooked meal. There are tried-and-true things you can do to set the mood, like candles and low lighting, romantic music (whether that's jazz or Sade), and a new outfit that makes you feel sexy. Valentine's Day is one of my favorite ways to break out of the winter blues and celebrate all the love in my life, whether it's the love I have for my husband or for my kids.

For us, Valentine's Day is also about the kids, and every year I try to decorate the kitchen table the night before so that when they come downstairs they get a Valentine's Day surprise.

I'll put out heart-shaped waffles or pancakes (you can do this easily with frozen waffles or pancakes and a cookie cutter). I also make them each a little basket filled with Valentine's candies and little gifts. Nothing fancy—you can get cute Valentine's gifts at any dollar store. I add books, heart-shaped glasses, Valentine's crafts, new crayons or markers, stickers, or necklaces they can wear. You can also surprise them while they're at school by sneaking little

Sample Valentine's Day Playlist

My love for music has no bounds, so I can go on and on . . . but below is a starter list.

"This Woman's Work" and/or "Fortunate" by Maxwell
"By Your Side" by Sade
"If I Ain't Got You" by Alicia Keys
"Water Runs Dry" by Boys II Men
"Lover" by Taylor Swift
"Nothing's Gonna Hurt You Baby" by Cigarettes After Sex
"No Woman No Cry" or "Is This Love" by Bob Marley
"Don't Know Why" by Norah Jones
"Tennessee Whiskey" by Chris Stapleton
"Kiss Me" by Ed Sheeran
"Purple Rain" by Prince
"He Loves Me" and/or "The Way" by Jill Scott
"Let It Be Me" by Ray LaMontagne

treats into their lunch boxes. One of my favorite things to do is carve heart shapes into their food. The red wax around Babybel cheese is a perfect canvas for a little surprise heart. If you use the tip of a sharp knife, you can draw hearts on a banana peel, and it will turn brown so they can see it at lunchtime. Or you can cut sandwiches and strawberries into heart shapes. I also leave little love notes in their backpacks.

Speaking of love notes, I feel like this is a tradition that has kind of taken a back seat to Instagram posts and hastily bought cards from the store, which—don't get me wrong—are better than nothing. But it's nice to bring a little romance to the holiday by taking the time to write out a love letter to your sweetie—using pen and paper, or even lipstick on his mirror.

Whether you write an epic poem worthy of Shakespeare or just jot down a few words to warm your partner's heart, writing a letter by hand makes the day much sweeter. You can also do this for friends, letting them know how much they mean to you and why you cherish your relationships with them. It's so rare to get a handwritten card these days that the gesture alone can make someone swoon, no matter how bad your handwriting has gotten over the years!

CHAPTER 22

A Silly Saint Patrick's Day

Believe it or not, Saint Patrick's Day is a winter holiday, since winter *technically* ends a few days after March 17. It's right on the cusp of spring, which is a pretty good excuse to celebrate, if you ask me.

Nick loves the holiday, mainly because it involves beer and it falls during March Madness, so we have a few traditions we keep alive every year as a way to make memories amid the chaos of school and work and the daily grind. We're definitely not heading out to a pub for shots and a beer, but we do indulge in some green food and drinks and uphold our own special tradition—a Saint Patrick's Day leprechaun dance party—or a jig, if you will.

For Camden, we had dance parties all the time. It was a spontaneous way to get silly and have some fun as a family. Then when the second and third babies came along, it was harder to keep the dance parties going, since bedtimes are scattered, but we try.

Over the years the Saint Patrick's Day dance party has become a way to connect as a family and have some holiday fun. Nick and I might pour ourselves a green beer or a regular Guinness, and I'll add green food coloring to the kids' lemonade to make "leprechaun punch."

Epic Saint Patrick's Day Fail

For Saint Patrick's Day in 2021, I decided it would be hilarious and festive to add some green food coloring to the toilet water plus two little green footprints on the seat to make it look like a leprechaun snuck in and peed in my kids' bathroom. Well, Cam and Phoenix thought it was hysterical, but poor Brooklyn was traumatized and refused to use that bathroom for three days because she thought a scary little green man had actually snuck in and peed. A few years before that, she was terrified by the sight of Nick in an Easter bunny suit, so I guess the lesson here is to know your audience, and your kids, before you pull a stunt like this.

Here are a few more ideas for turning this March holiday into something that's much more memorable than a night at a pub (although that sounds pretty good, too).

GREEN SHAMROCK-SHAPED RICE KRISPIES TREATS

LUCKY CHARMS IN THE MORNING WITH GREEN MILK

CAKE TOPPED WITH GREEN MARSHMALLOWS FROM THE LUCKY CHARMS BOX

CORNED BEEF HASH

KIWI MOJITOS

FOUR-LEAF-CLOVER-SHAPED CAKE OR COOKIES

SHEPHERD'S PIE POTATO SKINS

Nick's favorite breakfast to order at a restaurant is corned beef hash. If it's ever on a menu, he gets it. (That's how I am with a Cubano. If that sandwich is ever on a menu, you better believe I'm ordering it.) At home, I like to treat

Nick to a corned beef hash breakfast on Saint Patrick's Day, quickly followed by a Guinness.

A new tradition we started is called "catching a leprechaun." In Irish folklore, if you catch a leprechaun, he may grant you three wishes or lead you to his pot of gold. Most likely you won't catch one, because they are fast and clever, but they'll leave you gold chocolate coins for your effort. So Nick and I help the kids set leprechaun "traps" to try to catch them. Sometimes the leprechauns might even mess up some furniture or create mischief of their own by putting shamrock stickers on notebooks or mismatching your shoes or turning your milk green (with organic food coloring). They can stack chairs or wrap an area with string so you can't pass through. Let your imagination go wild! Think of things that would be fun for a child. Even though you're probably the one who's going to end up cleaning up the "leprechaun's" mess, it's worth it.

And Now, the Tradition Begins with YOU!

I hope you take all these tips and ideas as a gentle guide to creating a life that's all your own. Writing this book helped me see that I had a choice: I could become a victim of my childhood circumstances, or I could find strength in struggle and create a life full of love, beauty, and celebration (and as you probably can tell by now, I *love* a good party). That choice became a spark inside of me that continually nudges me to do more and be better, kinder, and more grateful every single day. In my mind, the only opinion that should matter is your own. How do *you* want to live your life? How do you see things playing out for you? It's yours for the taking.

When my kids look back on their lives, I hope they have happy memories, moments they will never forget, and smells and tastes that transport them back in time and make them smile. I want them to hear a song by Frank Sinatra and say, "My mom used to play this in the kitchen when she made her meat sauce." Maybe they encounter a jasmine-scented candle and remember the days I made them organize their toys for spring cleaning. No matter where you are in life, there is always room to create your own new traditions, and I would love to hear about the ones you're creating, so please share them with the hashtag #LifeFromScratchBook. The traditions in this book have become benchmarks in our family's life. At the end of the day, when I am old and gray and sitting on a porch with my husband, I hope we can have a glass of wine (or bourbon for Nick), kick back, and be proud of the life we created—from scratch.

PART 5

VANESSA'S CHICKEN ADOBO

Before you start cooking, please understand that mine is *not* the true Filipino way to make this dish! Trust me—I should know. I've gotten called out on social media several times. It took me several years and many iterations to come up with this version. Along the way a supportive (and always hungry) Nick would say, "Damn, baby!!! This is delicious! This is the *one!*" I've changed a few things over time to get to the current version. Like, I now use boneless, skinless chicken breasts along with the more traditional drumsticks and thighs. Also, I only use ground pepper because when I made the original recipe we were biting into cracked peppercorns that were so strong our eyes crossed. The point of this book, and of my sharing this recipe, is to inspire you to create your own traditions, whether they start with chicken adobo or homemade meatballs like your grandma made (but with your own special touch). Over time, this dish has become a vital part of our family traditions, and it was a huge inspiration for this book.

So to all the chicken adobo purists out there who might say this isn't the real deal: that's kind of the point. This recipe is *something* like the one my mother cooked, which made me feel warm and loved as we would sit together and eat it late at night. It has evolved into a dish that I cook for my husband and our three children as a way for us to sit together and have a meal (albeit not late at night).

I explain to my kids that it's a Filipino dish and tell them that I am (and they are) part Filipino. It's hard to tell if what I'm saying is sinking in or if they're just really into the food. I can't wait to see what dish my kids will think of when they think of home, but if I had to pick, I'd hope it would be this one.

I hope you love this recipe as much as I do, and I hope you make your own version and share it with a friend. If you come up with an amazing twist, share it with me on Instagram or Twitter with the hashtag #LifeFromScratchBook. Remember, this is all about creating your own traditions and memories, and I'd love to hear what you come up with.

2 tablespoons canola oil

4 bone-in, skin-on chicken thighs

4 bone-in, skin-on chicken drumsticks

2 large boneless, skinless chicken breasts

1 onion, cut into quarters and sliced

2 garlic cloves, minced

1 cup distilled white vinegar, or more if desired

1 cup low-sodium soy sauce, or more if desired

1 cup water, or more if desired

¼ to ½ teaspoon ground black pepper, or more if desired

3 bay leaves

Cooked white rice for serving

Heat the oil in a large skillet over medium-high heat. Add the chicken and cook until browned on both sides. FYI: This is a messy process with *lots* of grease splatter. As Nick's granny would say, "Wear a shirt when you're frying bacon!" Translation: *Don't cook naked.* It's solid advice, especially for this recipe. (I really wish I had the chance to cook with her in the kitchen. Fully clothed, of course.)

With your shirt still on, add the onion and garlic and cook for three or four minutes to release the flavors. Then add the vinegar, soy sauce, and water. Depending on how much chicken you have, you may need to add more of each. Add the black pepper (more if you like a kick) and bay leaves. Bring to a boil, reduce heat, and let simmer for 45 minutes to an hour.

I love that I can walk away and leave this on the stove so I can deal with three kids and a husband—who sometimes acts like a little kid himself (love you, honey!). I'll head back into the kitchen and turn over the chicken pieces once or twice, just so they soak in all the delicious flavors. Once the chicken is cooked through, serve it over rice.

Spring

VANESSA'S FAMOUS CHICKEN PASTA SALAD

My stepmom, Donna, didn't love cooking, but she had an arsenal of easy, quick side dishes to bring to a weekend BBQ. This one was always a favorite, and over the years I've changed a few ingredients here and there to personalize it.

I make it for BBQs and small get-togethers, and it's delicious the next day. You can make it ahead of time, which is key when you're trying to wrangle kids.

INGREDIENTS

1 pound medium pasta shells

1 12-ounce bottle Marie's Coleslaw Dressing (usually available in the produce aisle)

10 ounces canned all-white-meat chicken breast, drained

1 8-ounce block mild or sharp cheddar cheese, cubed

Salt and ground black pepper to taste

Fresh parsley for garnish (optional)

MAKING IT FROM SCRATCH . . .

Cook the shells according to package directions. Drain and allow to cool, then transfer to a serving bowl.

Add the dressing, chicken, cheese, and salt and pepper. Top with chopped parsley if you like. (My kids like it without. For parties a little color is a nice touch.)
Eat and enjoy!

EASTER DEVILED EGGS (AKA LACHEGGS)

This appetizer is a major hit in our family, and it's perfect for Easter or any spring event. Each year, my friends bring their own versions to our party, mainly because they know how much Nick adores them. Some friends pretty them up with food coloring. Others use creamy piped filling, but I've played around with my own recipe and come up with my favorite technique. Somehow, every Easter, our entire table of eggs gets eaten, and I think Nick is probably responsible for inhaling most of them.

Deviled eggs start with the perfect hard-boiled egg. I used to boil the egg, then spin it on the counter to test it—the old-school way. If it spun in place, it was ready. The problem was that I would always wonder why there were green bits in the egg and why the consistency was off. When I was on *Top Chef Junior*, the judges always taught the basics, and when they got into hard-boiled eggs, you better believe I was riveted. The key is the ice bath at the end. Who knew? Apparently, many people! It stops the cooking process so you get the perfect egg. You can boil the eggs for anywhere between four and twelve minutes, and after much experimentation I am a proud eleven-minute girl! I want them *done*.

MAKING THE PERFECT HARD-BOILED EGG

Place your eggs in the bottom of a saucepan. Be sure not to crowd them in the pan. They should fit comfortably.

Add cold water until it reaches an inch or so above the eggs.

Over high heat, bring the water to a boil, then cover the pan.

This is so important: remove from the heat and let the eggs sit in the hot water with the lid on. As I mentioned above, I leave mine for eleven minutes, resulting in the perfect consistency for my deviled eggs.

While the eggs are cooking, fill a large bowl with ice and add water. This ice bath will give you those perfect deviled eggs.

When the eggs are ready and your timer goes off, use tongs to remove the eggs from the hot water and place them gently into the ice bath. Don't drop them in and break them! Let them sit for about ten minutes.

Peel away the shells! I like doing this under running water to help get the tiny bits off.

Now you're ready to devil the eggs!

INGREDIENTS

6 hard-boiled eggs

1 tablespoon sweet pickle relish

3 tablespoons mayonnaise

1 teaspoon Dijon mustard

Salt and ground black pepper to taste

Thinly sliced sweet gherkin pickles for garnish

Paprika for garnish

MAKING IT FROM SCRATCH...

Cut the eggs in half lengthwise. Scoop out the yolks and place them in a medium mixing bowl. Add the relish, mayonnaise, mustard, and salt and pepper.

Spoon the yolk mixture into the whites (use a piping bag and pretty tip if you want that extra special touch), garnish some of the halves with one or two gherkin slices, and sprinkle all with paprika.

Pro tip: I like making the yolk mixture the day before and storing it in an airtight container. Then I fill and garnish right before guests arrive. I'm careful not to do this *too* early because Nick will eat them all before anyone else has a chance.

Mexican Fiesta

One of our favorite large-group spring meals is a fiesta, perfect for Cinco de Mayo or anytime you're in the mood for delicious Mexican flavors. You'll want guacamole, chips and salsa, an enchilada casserole, *all* the fixin's, and of course some margaritas and palomas or even just Coronas with lime. When you're entertaining, you don't want to be stuck stewing tomatoes for a sauce, so remember—canned goods are your friend!

GUACAMOLE

I know this is one of those "everyone knows how to make it" recipes, but here is how I prepare my simple and yummy six-ingredient guacamole, in case you want to mix it up (pun intended).

2 large ripe avocados: Smoosh the flesh in a medium-size bowl, then add the ingredients below.

1 cup small cherry tomatoes: These are a Lachey favorite. I quarter them with a serrated knife, since they are squishy and small. There's nothing worse than squirting tomatoes all over your kitchen.

Chopped cilantro: I know—some people think cilantro tastes like soap. If you hate it, leave it out, *but* I think it's necessary, so add as much (or as little) as you like. I use 1 tablespoon.

Chopped red onion: This is key for the crunch and punch of flavor. I add ¼ to ½ cup. It varies depending on the size of the avocados you use. But start with ¼ cup, and you can always add more.

Fresh lime juice: I cut a lime in half and squeeze all the goodness from both halves into the guacamole.

Salt to taste: I like to use coarse sea salt or kosher salt.

LACHEY LAYER DIP

After years of trying different versions of this beloved appetizer, we decided that this is our favorite. So many friends have emailed me asking for this particular recipe. It's just so yummy!

INGREDIENTS

1 16-ounce can refried beans

1 1-ounce package taco seasoning

8 ounces sour cream

4 ounces cream cheese, at room temperature

1 16-ounce jar prepared salsa

1 cup quartered cherry tomatoes or diced Roma tomatoes

¼ cup sliced scallions (optional)

1 8-ounce bag shredded lettuce

1 8-ounce bag shredded Mexican cheese blend

Sliced canned or jarred black olives for garnish

MAKING IT FROM SCRATCH . . .

In a small bowl, combine the beans and the taco seasoning. Spread into a 9 x 13-inch serving dish.

Combine the sour cream and softened cream cheese—I use half an 8-ounce block. If you need to put the cream cheese in the microwave to soften because you're making the dip at the last minute, don't put it in for too long. Just make it soft enough to blend.

Spread the sour cream mixture over the refried beans mixture as evenly as you can without combining the two layers in one big mush. At this point, you can let the dip sit in the refrigerator overnight. You don't want to add the lettuce and other layers this early because they'll get soggy. Also, if you're making the dip the day you're serving it, just let it chill in the fridge for 30 minutes to an hour so the flavors of the beans and taco seasoning can meld.

Next, add a layer of salsa. The whole jar! Then top with the tomatoes.

Sprinkle with the chopped scallions (I went through a no-scallions phase, and the dip was still yummy, but it's definitely better with them in there), followed by the shredded lettuce (yes, the whole bag), followed by the shredded cheese (yes, the whole bag).

Finally, add a pretty layer of sliced olives. You can get creative here with placement, but don't use too many, because they'll overwhelm the other flavors.

ENCHILADA CASSEROLE

I have always loved chicken-and-cheese enchiladas, but making them at home can be challenging. Maybe that's why I love casseroles! You can make them in advance *and* they're always consistent, since everything is combined in one big dish. Because of my desire to make enchiladas the *easy* way, my enchilada casserole was born. I always enlist Nick to help me shred the chicken while I assemble everything else, which gives us time together in the kitchen.

INGREDIENTS

4 boneless, skinless chicken breasts

1 tablespoon olive oil

1 cup chopped white onion

2 or 3 garlic cloves, minced, or ¼ teaspoon garlic powder if you're not up for mincing

1 10.5-ounce can condensed cream of celery soup

1 10.5-ounce can condensed cream of chicken soup

1 19-ounce can red enchilada sauce (we like mild, but you can get spicy!)

1 10-ounce can diced tomatoes with green chilies (hello, RO*TEL!), drained

1 4-ounce can diced green chilies, drained

½ teaspoon chili powder

16 mini yellow corn tortillas

1 16-ounce bag shredded Mexican cheese blend

Steam or boil the chicken breasts for about 18 minutes, then shred the meat with two forks. You want to make sure the chicken is feathery at the thickest part. I always cut into it and check. Sometimes I put it back in the water or steamer if it's not cooked enough.

Preheat the oven to 350°F.

Heat the oil in a skillet over medium-low heat. Cook the onions and garlic until the onions are soft and the flavors are combined, about 5 minutes. You don't want to overcook or brown the onions, just soften them.

In a large bowl, combine the soups, red enchilada sauce, tomatoes with green chilies, diced green chilies, cooked onions and garlic, and chili powder. (No chicken yet!) Spread 1 cup of the mixture in the bottom of a nonreactive 9 x 13-inch baking dish. Add the shredded chicken to the remaining liquid mixture in the bowl.

Layer 8 tortillas in the bottom of the dish. Top with half the chicken mixture, then half the cheese (about 2 cups).

Repeat the layers: 8 tortillas, the remaining chicken mixture, then the rest of the cheese.

Bake for 45 minutes to an hour, until the cheese is melted all over and the sides are bubbly. Cover with foil and let stand for 10 minutes before serving. Slice and enjoy!

PALOMAS

What's a Mexican fiesta without a paloma?

INGREDIENTS

½ cup blanco tequila

1 cup grapefruit juice (preferably freshly squeezed, but store-bought is yummy, too)

1 ounce freshly squeezed lime juice

¼ cup club soda or sparkling water

1 or 2 dashes simple syrup (don't overdo it if you use store-bought grapefruit juice!)

Lime slices for garnish

Mix all ingredients in a pitcher. Stir, pour over ice, garnish, and enjoy.

This is enough for me and Nick on fiesta night, but for a crowd, you can use the quantities below.

INGREDIENTS FOR PARTY PITCHER

2 cups blanco tequila

4 cups grapefruit juice

½ cup freshly squeezed lime juice

1 cup club soda or sparkling water

Simple syrup to taste (start with two or three drops, then go from there)

Summer

PULLED PORK

I registered for a Dutch oven when Nick and I got married, and I am obsessed with it. I use it often, and it makes such a difference. I guess you can say that Dutch-oven meals have become a tradition in our house. One weekend I wanted to try something new, so I found a pulled-pork recipe online and started playing around with it. I will say, since I didn't have a mother to teach me how to cook, the internet has *saved* me! One of my favorite things to do is read the comments sections in online recipes so I can see what other people think of a dish and how they'd modify it for their families. It's like the ultimate mom advice: tons of people have already made the recipe, and they share their mistakes and fixes with you. Plus, they're all regular kitchen cooks like me (as opposed to gourmet chefs), so the advice is always simple.

The Dutch oven does pretty much all the work in this recipe, so it's a win-win. You just prep it and let it cook. I make the rub and season the meat the day before. Then I put it in the oven in the morning, and by lunchtime it's ready to go.

INGREDIENTS

2 tablespoons salt

2 tablespoons ground black pepper

2 tablespoons dark brown sugar, firmly packed

2 tablespoons paprika

½ tablespoon cayenne pepper

4 pounds pork shoulder

2 cups apple juice

1 cup cider vinegar

2 tablespoons Worcestershire sauce

½ tablespoon liquid smoke (so important—I never knew it existed until I found this recipe!)

½ tablespoon garlic powder

Butter and brioche buns for serving

In a small bowl, combine the salt, pepper, brown sugar, paprika, and cayenne pepper. Rub the mixture all over the pork, gently pressing it into the meat. Cover and refrigerate for at least 2 hours or overnight.

In a medium bowl, combine the apple juice, vinegar, Worcestershire sauce, liquid smoke, and garlic powder. Pour the mixture into a Dutch oven, then add the pork and cover with foil. Roast for about 4 hours, until the pork pulls apart easily. Be sure to baste the pork with the liquid every hour or so.

Remove the roast from the oven and shred the pork with two forks or tongs.

Melt some butter in a skillet over medium heat. Slice the buns horizontally and place them in the skillet cut side down for a few minutes, until they're lightly toasted and golden.

Serve the pork on the buns with toppings of your choice!

CITRUS BEEF STIR-FRY

Nick loves Chinese food, and we ordered it all the time when he'd come visit me in New York (I was working on *Total Request Live* for MTV in those days). Some of my favorite memories are of us eating out of take-out boxes and sharing chopsticks—silly stuff that you think is so special and sexy when you're newly dating.

Fun fact: Nick's first job in LA when he was just starting out with 98 Degrees was delivering Chinese food in Burbank, California. One night in New York when we ordered food together, I wore sexy pajamas, plus full hair and makeup (I came from set on *TRL*). I went to answer the door, and he said, "I delivered Chinese food for years just waiting for someone to answer the door like that! This guy isn't getting it!" He made me go back to the room while he answered my door.

We moved into our first home together a month after our wedding, in August of 2011. Whenever I cooked, I loved making recipes "ours" by changing ingredients or celebrating things that were special to us. We had bought a wok together, and I wanted to make the first meal in our new home memorable, so I paid tribute to our Chinese takeout days by making this recipe from a Williams Sonoma cookbook we received as a wedding gift. Instead of tangerines, I used oranges, since they are always available and easy to get.

Nick loves this dish. If we're ever on a show like *The Newlywed Game*, I know what Nick will say when the host asks him, "Out of all the dishes Vanessa cooks for you, which one is your favorite?" There's a lot of work that goes into the prep, but it only takes a few minutes to cook, and it's so worth it. The original recipe called for minced fresh ginger, and I used to love making it, but now I just buy ginger paste to save a bit of time. I hope you try this recipe and love it as much as we do. I use 1 tablespoon regular soy sauce and 1 tablespoon dark soy sauce. If you can't find a Fresno chili pepper, substitute red bell peppers. It will be just as yummy!

INGREDIENTS

1½ pounds flank steak

¾ teaspoon granulated sugar, divided

¼ teaspoon baking soda

Salt to taste

1 teaspoon grated orange or tangerine zest

½ cup freshly squeezed orange or tangerine juice

1 tablespoon rice wine vinegar

1 tablespoon hoisin sauce

2 tablespoons soy sauce

1 teaspoon chili bean paste

1 teaspoon ginger paste

½ teaspoon sesame oil

¼ teaspoon cornstarch

4 tablespoons canola oil, divided

1 green bell pepper, seeded and thinly sliced

1 yellow onion, thinly sliced

1 Fresno chili pepper, seeded and thinly sliced

2 garlic cloves, minced

Rice, cooked according to package instructions

MAKING IT FROM SCRATCH . . .

Cut the flank steak into slices that are about ⅛ inch thick. Place the slices in a bowl and toss with ½ teaspoon sugar, baking soda, and salt. Let sit for at least half an hour at room temperature.

To make the sauce (this is the time-consuming part!), whisk the citrus zest and juice, rice wine, hoisin sauce, soy sauce, chili bean paste, ginger paste, sesame oil, remaining ¼ teaspoon sugar, and cornstarch together in a small bowl. When the sugar and cornstarch dissolve, you're ready for the next step.

Gently pat the beef dry with a paper towel. In a wok or large skillet, heat 2 tablespoons of the canola oil over high heat. Add a layer of beef, searing it on one side for about a minute. Flip the meat and sear it on the other side for about 30 seconds. Put the beef in a colander to drain and repeat the process with the remaining beef.

Quickly wipe out the wok with a paper towel, then heat the remaining 2 tablespoons of canola oil over high heat. Stir-fry the bell pepper and onion for about 3 minutes, then stir in the chili pepper and garlic. Stir-fry for about one minute. By this point, your house will smell a-*mazing*! Next, pour in the reserved sauce, then add the beef, cooking until the sauce thickens, 1 to 2 minutes. Place all that yumminess on a serving plate along with rice and enjoy.

LACHEY LOBSTER ROLLS

It was an ordinary day on *Top Chef Junior*, and I was in the kitchen watching a bunch of young kids cook lobster. I couldn't help but think two things: one, what an amazing opportunity we're giving these kids who love cooking. And two, if a kid can cook lobster, damn it, I can, too.

I will never forget when one of our young chefs said she had never felt more normal and welcomed by other people than she did on our set. She always felt like an outcast at home because most girls her age were into other things, and all she wanted to do was cook. She said she finally felt like she had peers her age who were also into spices, umami flavors, and learning how to sous-vide a duck and that she didn't feel so "weird." I completely melted. I was so happy to see this little girl find her way and meet other kids who shared her love of cooking. Some people see cooking as a chore, but others discover joy in it. So as I watched these kids make the most amazing dishes, I got inspired.

There was a lot of lobster left over after that shoot because the task for that day was to humanely cook one. Who knew you could do it humanely, with no screams? I immediately asked Jamie, the head of the culinary department at the show, what I could do with the lobster, and she suggested lobster rolls. You just add some onion, celery, lemon juice and zest, mayo, and crème fraîche to bind. Of course I panicked and asked her for measurements and cooking time. That's the thing about chefs—they usually wing it and leave measurements to the non-pros. For them, cooking is an art, and you can ditch the measurements and just *feel it*, if you will. So I went home, lobster tails and other ingredients in hand.

The next day, Nick had some friends over to watch sports, and I decided to surprise them with my "kids-can-do-it-and-so-can-I" dish. There were four guys, so I thought, okay, four tails equals four sandwiches. I literally used a handful of this and a handful of that, a dash of this and a dash of that. I prayed it would turn out okay. But if there's anything I've learned on *Top Chef Junior*, other than to clean my cooking station, it's to *taste* as you cook! And lemme tell you, it tasted delicious.

I toasted the buns, served them up, and I have never had a quicker positive reaction. That was years ago, and to this day an ongoing joke with Nick's friends is that if I love you, I will make you my lobster rolls. There is a good amount of prep involved, but the results are so worth it! As I was putting this book together, Nick and his friends piped in with, "V, the lobster rolls *have* to be in there!"

So here you go. This is something special that has become a Lachey staple. And don't panic: I *am* giving you measurements. You can also play with the ingredients yourself. Want more crunch? Add more celery. Want more citrus? Add more zest. Make it your own! 'Cause this one is mine, and I love that I can share it with you!

INGREDIENTS

4 frozen lobster tails (about 4 ounces each)

Mayonnaise to taste

2 tablespoons crème fraîche

1 tablespoon chopped chives

1 teaspoon chopped fresh tarragon or ¼ teaspoon dried tarragon

¼ cup finely chopped red onion

¼ cup finely chopped celery

Zest of 1 lemon (really elevates flavor!)

1 tablespoon freshly squeezed lemon juice (maybe less; you don't want it runny)

½ teaspoon Old Bay Seasoning

Salt and ground black pepper to taste

Ghee or butter

4 brioche buns

Chopped flat-leaf parsley for garnish

MAKING IT FROM SCRATCH . . .

Steam the lobster tails for 6 to 12 minutes. Immediately plunge them into an ice bath to stop the cooking. Allow the lobster tails to cool, then drain, remove the shells, chop the meat, and set aside.

In a large bowl, combine the mayonnaise, crème fraîche, chives, tarragon, onion, celery, lemon zest and juice, Old Bay Seasoning, and salt and pepper. Add the lobster, mix well, and refrigerate for at least 30 minutes.

Melt the ghee in a large skillet. Place the buns in the skillet cut side down for a few minutes, until they're lightly toasted and golden. If you want you can hollow out a roll as shown (or if your local store doesn't have the bread you need), but my favorite way is a toasted brioche bun.

Spoon the lobster mixture into the buns, top with parsley, and serve with chips and a cold beer!

NICKY'S NECTAR

One of my favorite things to do when I plan a party with my girl Corrie is think of a specialty drink with our go-to guy John. I always think about the guest of honor or occasion and go from there. This one was created for Nick on Father's Day. I wanted something refreshing but also with a "Nick kick."

INGREDIENTS

1 ounce Rittenhouse rye

1 ounce Cynar

½ ounce freshly squeezed lemon juice

½ ounce ginger simple syrup (available online)

1 ounce India pale ale

MAKING IT FROM SCRATCH . . .

In a cocktail shaker, combine the rye, Cynar, lemon juice, ginger syrup, and ale. Shake vigorously for 5 to 10 seconds *without* ice. Hold the shaker tightly closed, because the contents will be under pressure from the IPA. The shaking creates foam and mimics the effect of an egg white. Open the shaker and add a scoop of ice. Close the shaker and shake vigorously for 5 to 10 seconds to chill. Then strain the contents into the other side of the shaker and discard the ice. Now that the contents are cold, shake again *without* ice for another 5 to 10 seconds. Strain into a rocks glass or coupe. The cocktail will be cloudy and will separate in the glass.

Enjoy!

FLANK STEAK

In chapter 10, I talked about Nick's grilling skills (love you, babe). But I will say that one thing he does *not* mess up is our flank steak. Here's how he does it.

INGREDIENTS

⅓ cup olive oil

2 garlic cloves, minced

2 tablespoons red wine vinegar

⅓ cup soy sauce

¼ cup honey

½ teaspoon ground black pepper

2 to 3 pounds flank steak

MAKING IT FROM SCRATCH . . .

In a large nonreactive bowl, combine the olive oil, garlic, vinegar, soy sauce, honey, and pepper. Add the flank steak and cover with clear plastic wrap. Refrigerate at least 1 hour or, even better, overnight. Turn the meat once if you can. You can also put the meat and marinade in a large ziplock bag so all the juices get soaked up. Just put the bag in a bowl or on a plate in case it leaks.

When you're ready to cook, take the bowl out of the refrigerator and it let sit at room temperature for about 30 minutes.

Heat the grill to 400 degrees.

Remove the meat from the marinade and grill it over direct heat for 3 minutes per side. Then move the meat off the direct heat and grill it for 4 minutes per side.

Take the steak off the grill, cover with foil, and let it rest for 5 minutes. Don't cut into it right away! Then thinly slice the meat against the grain. I like the ends, which are a little more done, and Nick likes the middle.

JALAPEÑO POPPER SPREAD

Nick is the king of saying, "Hey, babe? I have some friends coming over. In an hour." Not gonna lie: I may roll my eyes at times, but in the end I always love entertaining. I want our house to be the house where my kids and their friends want to hang out, which means I always need to have snacks on hand.

Over the years I've kicked up my dips a notch, and this one is Nick's favorite. When he springs get-togethers on me, I'm always armed with a dip. Also, you can halve the recipe if you want to make it for a smaller occasion, like a double-date night.

INGREDIENTS

2 8-ounce packages cream cheese, softened

1 cup mayonnaise

½ cup shredded Monterey Jack cheese

1 4-ounce can diced jalapeño peppers, drained

1 4-ounce can diced green chilies, drained

1 5-ounce can all-white-meat chicken breast, drained (optional)

1 cup shredded Parmesan cheese

½ cup panko

MAKING IT FROM SCRATCH...

Preheat the oven to 400°F.

Place the cream cheese in a microwave-safe bowl and heat it for 15 to 20 seconds on medium power. Take it out and stir so the middle gets as warm as the outer edges. Repeat the process if necessary until the cream cheese melts. Stir in the mayonnaise, Monterey Jack, jalapeños, green chilies, and chicken (if using). Spread the mixture evenly into a 9 x 13-inch baking dish. Top with the Parmesan, then with the panko.

Bake for 25 to 30 minutes. Cool and serve with crackers, bagel chips, or tortilla chips.

MINNILLO BEANS

As I said, my stepmom, Donna, didn't like to cook. We joked that she was the queen of the microwave. But one day out of nowhere she made these amazing non-microwave beans. She later told me that she got the recipe from one of my dad's air force friends who made them for a party in Charleston.

I have so much respect for my dad's time in the military. The camaraderie he shared with his fellow airmen ran deep: they worked together and played together, and there was a party or event almost every weekend. If you didn't go to a party, you *had* to host the next one. And they had a funny way of telling you: you would come home one day after the party you missed, and your yard would be full of pink plastic flamingos. I guess that's military party etiquette—or at least it was among my dad's buddies. I remember coming home one day from school and being mortified to see dozens of plastic flamingos in our yard. In retrospect, I got an amazing recipe out of the fiasco, so it was worth a little teen angst!

This was my first glimpse into the practice of sharing recipes and spreading the love as opposed to hoarding them like a mean old-school grandmother who doesn't tell you all the ingredients on purpose—or who develops "recipe amnesia" when you ask her how to make something. These beans are great for a crowd, so when Nick and I were getting ready to host our first summer BBQ, I asked Donna for her recipe. I can't believe I never made them earlier in life. I guess I was too busy trying to find my place in the world rather than hosting parties! It's so simple, and because I was a novice cook at the time, it was the perfect way to wow the crowd without a lot of effort. That little burst of confidence was all I needed to keep on cooking . . .

1 28-ounce can baked beans

1 16-ounce can kidney beans, drained

1 16-ounce can lima beans, drained

1 ¼ pounds lean ground turkey, browned and drained

10 slices turkey bacon, cooked and chopped into bite-size pieces

½ cup ketchup

2 tablespoons white vinegar

¾ cup brown sugar, firmly packed

1 cup chopped white onion

MAKING IT FROM SCRATCH . . .

Preheat the oven to 325°F.

In a large bowl, combine all ingredients. Pour into a casserole dish and bake for two hours. Alternatively, transfer to a slow cooker and cook for four hours on low.

Over the years I have tweaked the recipe a bit and made it my own. Donna's recipe called for ground beef, for example, but I substituted turkey. I made these for Nick's grandmother for her eightieth birthday party, and *that* was when she started to warm up to me. It wasn't until she tried the Minnillo beans that our relationship truly began. Food can help solve any issue! That and a good bottle of wine.

I always assemble these beans the night before and just pop them in the oven the next day if it's a sit-down meal. I use the slow cooker if it's a BBQ-and-pool kind of day so that people can graze for hours. It's a great summer dish *and* a great way to win over a skeptical grandma.

Fall

V'S GAME-DAY CHILI

This is one of my go-to fall recipes because it pairs perfectly with . . . football season. On Sundays, Nick is pretty much out of commission and glued to not one but several TVs, watching games with his friends (the Bengals are his team, but he watches them all). When we were younger, we would go to bars and watch games all day, but as we got older, we started a tradition of having his buddies over to the house. As I mentioned earlier, his friends know they can come over any Sunday during the fall for football and chili and beer. Honestly, it's pretty good prep for having teenage boys in the house one day.

This chili is a staple because it can sit in a slow cooker all day and stay warm, whether people want to eat it during kickoff, at halftime, or after the game to celebrate (or forget that their team just lost).

INGREDIENTS FOR THE CHILI

2 pounds lean ground turkey, browned in canola oil and drained

1 white onion, chopped

1 red bell pepper, seeded and chopped

1 green bell pepper, seeded and chopped

Salt and ground black pepper to taste

1 16-ounce can kidney beans, drained

1 16-ounce can black beans, drained

1 28-ounce can crushed tomatoes

1 15-ounce can petite diced tomatoes, with liquid

1 6-ounce can tomato paste

1 teaspoon ground cumin

1 teaspoon dried oregano

1 teaspoon paprika

1 teaspoon chili powder

½ teaspoon cayenne pepper

Shredded cheese, diced onion or sliced scallions, and sour cream

MAKING IT FROM SCRATCH . . .

Combine the chili ingredients in a slow cooker and cook on high for 4 hours, stirring occasionally.

I usually put this together in the morning, so that by noon, when our guests are hungry, it's ready to go. By late afternoon it's still good if you leave it in the slow cooker on warm.

Serve with shredded cheese, some diced onion or sliced scallions, and a dollop of sour cream on top.

COZY BEEF STEW

Like most people, Nick is a sucker for a cozy home-cooked meal. And I am all about comfort food. I definitely think that we need to make healthy choices when it comes to eating and exercising, but for me, "cheat days" and cozy comfort meals here and there are 100 percent worth it. The first time I made this beef stew for Nick was during March Madness one year when the Cincinnati Bearcats were in the Sweet 16. (If you're not a sports fanatic like my husband, I'm talking about college basketball.) He loved it so much that he told me to save the recipe, and it's become one of our favorite fall dishes to make. It's perfect on a cool or cold night. My kids are huge fans now, too.

This one takes time, but that's also one of my favorite things about it. I'm all for keeping things quick and simple, but sometimes it's nice to savor the experience of cooking. The kids want to be in the kitchen, and Nick sneaks in and steals bites of meat while I cook. I get to hang with the family and enjoy some music and wine while prepping. I start this early because it needs to cook for a long time. I've changed a few things over the years to make it ours.

INGREDIENTS

3 to 4 pounds boneless beef chuck, cubed (I buy it precut for ease)

Salt and ground black pepper to taste

2 tablespoons canola oil

6 to 8 slices thick-cut bacon, chopped (this is important because the grease from the bacon is what you cook with)

1 cup chopped onion

1 cup chopped carrots (I like to use sliced or diced baby carrots)

1 cup chopped celery

2 garlic cloves, minced

2 tablespoonsdunsalted butter

6 tablespoons all-purpose flour

4 cups (1 32-ounce box) beef stock or beef broth

2 tablespoons tomato paste

1 tablespoon chopped flat-leaf parsley

1 teaspoon fresh thyme leaves (fresh herbs kick up the flavor)

1 teaspoon fresh rosemary leaves

1 bay leaf

1 ½ pounds small unpeeled red-skinned potatoes, quartered (I buy the tiny ones in a bag)

Cooked rice for serving

MAKING IT FROM SCRATCH . . .

Position a rack in the lower third of the oven. Preheat to 325°F.

Lay the cut beef on a cookie sheet and generously season with salt and pepper. Set aside.

In a large Dutch oven, heat the oil over medium heat. Add the chopped bacon, stirring occasionally until browned, about 7 minutes. Using tongs, transfer the bacon to a paper-towel-lined plate and set aside.

Drain the bacon grease into a glass bowl or measuring cup. Return 2 tablespoons of the grease to the pot and heat over medium-high heat. Add just enough beef to cover the bottom of the pot (this might take a few batches). You want each piece touching the bottom. Cook for 5 to 7 minutes, turning the meat to make sure all sides get browned. Transfer to a rack set over a cookie sheet to drain while you brown the rest of the beef.

Once all the beef is browned, pour another 2 tablespoons of bacon fat into the Dutch oven and heat over medium heat. Add the onion, carrot, celery, and garlic. Cook for 5 minutes, stirring constantly. Add the butter and stir. Once the butter is melted, add the flour. Keep stirring. (This part goes quickly, so it's wise to have everything prepped before cooking.) Gradually stir in the stock, about a cup at a time. Mix until combined and pasty, and keep adding and mixing. Once it's all mixed in, stir in the tomato paste, then add the parsley, thyme, rosemary, and bay leaf. Return the beef to the pot and bring to a slow boil. Cover tightly, transfer to the oven, and cook for 90 minutes.

Remove the stew from the oven and place the pot on the stove over medium heat. Add the potatoes. (The potatoes should not be too large, because if they are, they won't cook fully.) Replace the lid and simmer for 45 minutes.

Serve over rice, sprinkling the reserved bacon pieces on top. We usually have to grab our bacon quickly, because Brooklyn has become a bacon bandit. She steals it and eats it before we can even reach for it!

GROWN-UP MAC & CHEESE

There are so many varieties of this classic dish now. There's creamy mac, made with a roux base, and bricklike mac that reminds me of being a kid. There's mac with meat, veggie mac, lobster mac, and French onion mac. Over the years I've played with this recipe, trying different cheeses, adding ham and bell peppers, and sometimes using a different base. I always come back to the fact that a roux is the ultimate base for creamy mac and cheese. And trust me—I've tried them all.

Fun fact: the first time I made this I had to google "roux." The recipe just said to make your own roux, and being a newbie cook I had no clue what that meant. Basically, roux is a butter-and-flour mixture used as a base for sauces. For this recipe, I make it before adding the milk. You have to either use warm milk or add it slowly, otherwise you will end up with big clumps of flour. Yuck. Make sure you let the butter-and-flour mixture cook for a few minutes, too, to prevent your mac and cheese from tasting like chalk (the flour taste has to burn off).

INGREDIENTS

Kosher salt

1 pound elbow macaroni

4 cups whole milk

6 tablespoons unsalted butter

½ cup all-purpose flour

½ teaspoon ground black pepper

1 4-ounce can diced jalapeño peppers, drained

12 ounces grated Gruyère cheese

8 ounces grated pepper Jack cheese

Preheat the oven to 375°F.

Bring a large pot of water to a boil over high heat. Add a generous amount of kosher salt. I mean, salt it! It should taste like the ocean in there. Add the macaroni and cook according to package directions. Drain, rinse quickly, and set aside.

Warm the milk in a saucepan over medium-low heat, but do not boil. This makes it easier to blend with the roux. Cold milk won't work.

Melt the butter in large stainless steel pot (one that won't scratch—I don't want you to hate me afterward). This will be the pot in which your mac and cheese comes together in the end. Add the flour and cook, whisking constantly, for two minutes.

While whisking, gradually add the warm milk, a cup or less at a time. As it thickens up, add more, whisking constantly. Important! Don't add all of the milk at once.

Remove the pan from the heat, then add the pepper and jalapeños and stir. Add the cheeses and stir again. (I like to use a silicone spatula spoon, not a whisk.) Add the macaroni and stir again.

Pour the mixture into a greased 9 x 13-inch baking dish and bake for 30 to 35 minutes, until bubbly. Enjoy!

Winter

LACHEY LASAGNA

This is my favorite thing to make for a large crowd or to give to a new mama, because when you're going on two hours of sleep after feeding, changing, and burping a newborn, you can barely remember the *word* for lasagna, let alone how to make it. During any season, this recipe is always a crowd pleaser, but it's an especially good way to warm up after a cold winter day. Bonus: you can save the leftover sauce to make another dish later. The unpredictable chaos that is life with young kids has led me to love simple recipes like this. Plus, even though it's easy to cook, it makes you *feel* like a chef, since you can say, "Hey, I'm cooking with fennel seeds and basil."

INGREDIENTS

1 pound sweet Italian turkey sausage, casings removed

1 pound lean ground turkey (I use the 1-pound Jennie-O packs)

½ cup chopped or minced white onion

2 garlic cloves, crushed or minced

1 28-ounce can crushed tomatoes

1 12-ounce can tomato paste

1 15-ounce can tomato sauce

½ cup water

2 tablespoons granulated sugar

1½ teaspoons dried basil

½ teaspoon fennel seeds

1 teaspoon Italian seasoning

1 tablespoon salt, plus more as needed

¼ teaspoon ground black pepper

4 tablespoons chopped flat-leaf parsley, divided

12 lasagna noodles, or more or fewer to taste

1 15-ounce tub ricotta cheese

1 egg

¾ pound presliced low-moisture mozzarella cheese, divided

¾ cup grated Parmesan cheese, divided

In a large dry Dutch oven, brown the sausage over medium heat, breaking it up into a crumble as you go. When it's almost brown, add the ground turkey. When the meat is fully cooked, add the onion and garlic and sauté until the onion is translucent. Then add the crushed tomatoes, tomato paste, and tomato sauce. Add the water and mix well. Next, add the sugar, basil, fennel, Italian seasoning, salt, pepper, and 2 tablespoons of the parsley.

Simmer, covered, for 90 minutes (or more). I like this because it doesn't require an exact time, so if I'm cooking and Camden throws a ball in the house that hits a vase and makes water spill all over Brooklyn's dress while Phoenix simultaneously needs a diaper change, the lasagna doesn't get ruined. When you have kids, the romantic process of cooking at a leisurely pace while sipping wine isn't always realistic, so "simple and easy" is my go-to style. This sauce requires only that you simmer it and occasionally stir and taste.

Cheat trick: at this point, if I'm too busy, or if I just don't feel like assembling the lasagna, I'll put some of this sauce over spaghetti, and *boom*! Dinner is served. I save the rest of the sauce and assemble the lasagna the next day.

You can also freeze a small portion of the sauce, and when you're in a pinch, put that frozen chunk in a pot on the stove over low heat. It works for all sorts of pastas, and it will warm up nicely and no one will know it's not fresh!

Okay, back to the lasagna . . .

Bring a large pot of salted water to a boil. Cook the lasagna noodles according to the package directions. Then drain the noodles and rinse under cold water. At this point, I lay them out on a cookie sheet so I can easily grab them as I'm assembling.

In a medium bowl, mix the ricotta with the egg. Add the remaining 2 tablespoons of parsley and salt to taste.

Preheat oven to 375°F.

Spread 1½ cups of the meat sauce on the bottom of a 9 x 13-inch casserole dish. Place half the noodles on top of the sauce in an overlapping layer. (I use six of them in this step.) Spread with half the ricotta cheese mixture. Then top with half the mozzarella cheese

slices in an even layer (cut the slices to fit if you have to). Next, add another 1½ cups of the meat sauce, then sprinkle with ¼ cup of the Parmesan.

Repeat the layers, starting with the noodles, then the ricotta mixture, then the mozzarella. Top with 1½ cups sauce and the remaining ½ cup Parmesan cheese. If you have sauce leftover, save it for another use.

Cover the dish tightly with foil and bake for 25 minutes. Remove the foil, then bake for an additional 25 minutes.

I like bringing this to families along with a ready-to-assemble Caesar salad. I just put precut bagged lettuce, croutons, Caesar dressing, and cheese in a bag. Add a box of frozen garlic bread, and bring some dessert, like cookies from a local bakery (or you can bring homemade cookies if you're a magical unicorn with lots of free time). You can also bring fruit for the kids. A nice bottle of red wine is the cherry on top. This is the most thoughtful thing you can give a family with a new baby or a person who's going through a crazy or stressful time—the gift of a home-cooked meal. I know we can all order out, but sometimes you just want comfort food made with love.

LIFE FROM SCRATCH IN ACTION

What Is Mise en Place?

On *Top Chef Junior* I learned the term *mise en place*, which is a French cooking term that means "putting in place." Once I heard it, I realized I was already kind of doing it. It's all about preparation—it means getting everything measured and prepped and ready so that the actual cooking process can be stress-free. My lasagna recipe is one that definitely benefits from a little *mise en place*.

CHEESY HASH BROWNS

If you've ever taken a road trip across the country, especially through the South, then you've pulled over and had cheesy *something*! You can get bacon, eggs, cheesy hash browns, and a stack of pancakes on the side.

One of my favorite meals to eat out is breakfast because it's savory and sweet—it's meat and potatoes and veggies and, yes, cheese! But with three kiddos, eating out for breakfast isn't as fun, plus I'm usually still in my robe and haven't brushed my hair or teeth until the kids have eaten. So I created this recipe for southern "road-trip-inspired" cheesy hash browns because I wanted a yummy breakfast spread for my family—something that, on weekends, can bring us together at the table (just not at a roadside diner).

I take the time to cook the onions in the butter before I combine them with the rest of the ingredients because the kids are very into texture, and they don't like the crunch of an onion in their cheesy potatoes. Yes, there are all kinds of ways people have re-created hash browns, but this is our favorite!

INGREDIENTS

½ cup (1 stick) unsalted butter

½ cup chopped white onion

1 10.5-ounce can condensed cream of chicken soup

16 ounces sour cream

¼ teaspoon ground black pepper

1 30-ounce bag frozen hash brown potatoes

2 cups shredded Colby Jack cheese, divided

MAKING IT FROM SCRATCH . . .

Preheat the oven to 350°F.

Melt the butter in a pan set over medium to medium-low heat. You don't want to burn the butter or overcook the onions. This is just to soften them for the dish.

Add the onion and cook, stirring constantly, for 5 minutes. Make sure they don't brown. Turn the heat down if you need to. A nice frothy bubbling in the pan is perfect. Remove from the heat and set aside.

In a large bowl, combine the soup, sour cream, and pepper. Add the hash browns. Right from the freezer is fine! I throw the bag on the counter a few times to loosen the potatoes.

Add the onion mixture and mix well. I use a spatula to scrape the sides while mixing so nothing is wasted or left in the bowl. Add 1½ cups Colby Jack and mix again.

Pour the mixture into a greased 9 x 13-inch baking dish. Top with the remaining ½ cup Colby Jack.

Bake, uncovered, for 45 minutes. Let cool and enjoy! The leftovers are yummy the next day, too.

MONKEY BREAD

Monkey bread is a kid favorite in our household, but it's also a Nick favorite! When a friend realized I was making biscuits and pancakes and cutting them into small pieces, she said, "You should try monkey bread! The kids will love the pieces." I had never heard of it. I thought it must have been bite-size banana bread or something. Nope—*better*! It's cinnamon-and-sugar biscuits baked in a cake pan with a butter-and-brown-sugar glaze. To eat them, you just pull them apart. Pure deliciousness. It's a great sweet option next to savory casseroles when you have a large brunch get-together. I started with a Pillsbury recipe and then played with the ingredients to make it my own.

INGREDIENTS

½ cup granulated sugar

1 teaspoon ground cinnamon

2 16.3-ounce cans Pillsbury Grands! Flaky Layers Original Biscuits, chilled

½ cup raisins

1 cup brown sugar, firmly packed

¾ cup (1 ½ sticks) melted butter

MAKING IT FROM SCRATCH . . .

Preheat the oven to 350°F.

Grease a 12-cup Bundt pan with cooking spray. In a large (gallon-size) ziplock bag, mix the granulated sugar and cinnamon.

Separate the dough into 16 biscuits; cut each into quarters. Shake the biscuits in the bag to coat with the sugar mixture. Arrange the biscuits in the pan, distributing the raisins evenly among the biscuit pieces. Sprinkle any remaining sugar mixture over the biscuits.

In small bowl, mix the brown sugar and butter, then pour the mixture over the biscuit pieces.

Bake for 30 to 40 minutes, or until the bread is golden brown and no longer doughy in the center. Gently loosen the bread away from the edges of the pan with a spatula. Cool 5 minutes, then turn the pan upside down onto a serving plate. If any biscuit pieces or caramel remain in the pan, replace them on the bread. Serve warm.

BROOKLYN'S BRUNCH CASSEROLE

I have made the same breakfast casserole for Christmas morning ever since Nick and I spent our first winter holiday together. We started dating during the summer of 2006, and that December it was just the two of us at his house in California. It was actually the first Christmas I'd spent with a significant other, and I wanted to make something special for Christmas morning—something that didn't require a ton of work so we could relax and snuggle in bed and I wouldn't be stressed out trying to make something crazy like a soufflé! That's how the tradition started (basically, with me wanting to snuggle), and it has evolved over time. I change the bottom layer each year—sometimes it's biscuits; sometimes it's potatoes; sometimes it's crescent rolls—but it's always delicious and easy. Instead of slaving away over homemade biscuits, I started using store-bought, and that way Brooklyn can help me cook by laying out the biscuits, as I mentioned earlier. It makes her feel so proud, and she's now part of the tradition, which I love.

Brooklyn is a girl after my own heart. She loves cooking, entertaining, and taking care of everyone. She also loves her sweet tea and biscuits! When I lived in Charleston, South Carolina, as a child, I learned to love southern staples like these. It's so special for me to be able to introduce these little culinary memories to my kids.

INGREDIENTS

1 pound breakfast sausage patties or links

½ white onion, chopped

1 16.3-ounce can Pillsbury Grands! Southern Homestyle Buttermilk Biscuits

6 eggs, well beaten

¼ to ½ cup whole milk

Salt and ground black pepper to taste

8 ounces shredded cheese blend of your choice

Preheat the oven to 350°F.

In a large dry skillet, brown the sausage over medium heat, breaking it up into a crumble as you go. Do not drain.

Add the onion and sauté until translucent, about 5 minutes. (You can prepare the recipe up to this point the night before if you want to save time in the morning.)

Separate the dough into 8 biscuits; cut each into quarters. Arrange the pieces in a greased 9 x 13-inch baking dish. Bake for 8 minutes. (The biscuits won't be fully cooked at this point.) Remove from the oven and sprinkle the sausage-and-onion mixture over the top.

In a medium bowl, combine the eggs, milk, and salt and pepper, then pour the mixture over the entire dish. Bake for 15 minutes.

Remove the dish from the oven, sprinkle the cheese on top, then cook an additional 5 minutes. Let cool for 5 minutes before serving.

This will definitely warm you up during the winter months, and it's just as good the next day or as a late-night snack with ketchup. (Yes, ketchup!)

Acknowledgments

They say it takes a village, and that's the truth! I'm proud to also call my village my family, and I can never thank them enough for supporting me in this journey of life, but here goes . . .

To my team! This would *not* have been possible without you.

Ashley Josephson, over the fifteen years that we have been together (since before we met in my baseball hat and jeans), I have had this dream and you have *never* given up on me. Through a ton of "no's" and many versions later, WE DID IT! I adore you as a woman, friend, mother, and manager. Thank you for always leading my team with a huge heart and getting things *done*. I'm truly the luckiest to have you, and yes, I will follow you *anywhere*!

Brandi Bowles—finally, a book agent who got me! Thank you for putting the dream team together and making us hustle.

Hilary Swanson, my fairy bookmother! You believed in me the second you saw my proposal and got HarperOne to believe in me, too. Through a lockdown quarantine, your pregnancy, and my homeschool nightmare, you managed to lovingly push me through every deadline. Your compassion for my story is what got us here. I can't wait for all of *your* family traditions that you and Dan will create with Elliot. He's a lucky boy!

Dina Gachman, my co-writer. Through tons of emails, texts, FaceTimes, more texts, phone calls, more texts, coffee, Zooms, a Texas winter storm with no power on deadline week, and more texts, you have had the hardest job of all! Putting my brain, vision, love, and ideas into words. Thank you for co-piloting this crazy flight and getting me down on the page! You are a *rock* star mama, and I will always be indebted to you.

Justin Coit, you literally brought my book to life! From our very first shoot when I became a new mom with one baby to a decade later with a book and family of five (with two fur babies and fish and guinea pigs), I have loved having you along for the journey. You know how to capture our family and our essence, and I will forever be grateful to have these memories to cherish.

Kate Martindale, your passion, vision, and crazy organization matched me equally! Thank you for pulling a lifetime together in less than a week, all with an infectious smile and good glass of wine!

Ashlee Clay, Liz Castellanos, and Sonja Christensen—my pretty committee. Yes, it's always what's on the inside that counts, but damn, you make a gal feel good on the outside, too! I love you girls!

To Corrie Mendes, thank you for making every celebration in my life a special moment to remember forever. It's the little things, right? I love and adore you and am so grateful for our friendship! From my wedding to babies and beyond!

To all the moms I learned from, the friends who held my hand through good times and bad, the countless articles online and comments from strangers who helped make me a better mom, woman, and version of myself: I am so thankful to surround myself with friends I can call family. Thank you for making me believe in myself and allowing me to be strong enough to create a life for *my family*—one we curated all on our own.

And most importantly, my parents: Dad, thanks for the love you gave and the sacrifices you made so I could follow my heart. My stepmom, Donna, thank you for showing me that it's never too late for new beginnings. You are the best Nona my kids can ask for. I love you both and am inspired because of YOU!

Universal Conversion Chart

OVEN TEMPERATURE EQUIVALENTS

250°F = 120°C
275°F = 135°C
300°F = 150°C
325°F = 160°C
350°F = 180°C
375°F = 190°C
400°F = 200°C
425°F = 220°C
450°F = 230°C
475°F = 240°C
500°F = 260°C

MEASUREMENT EQUIVALENTS

Measurements should always be level unless directed otherwise.

⅛ teaspoon = 0.5 mL
¼ teaspoon = 1 mL
½ teaspoon = 2.5 mL
1 teaspoon = 5 mL
1 tablespoon = 3 teaspoons = ½ fluid ounce = 15 mL
2 tablespoons = ⅛ cup = 1 fluid ounce = 30 mL
4 tablespoons = ¼ cup = 2 fluid ounces = 60 mL
5⅓ tablespoons = ⅓ cup = 3 fluid ounces = 80 mL
8 tablespoons = ½ cup = 4 fluid ounces = 120 mL
10⅔ tablespoons = ⅔ cup = 5 fluid ounces = 160 mL
12 tablespoons = ¾ cup = 6 fluid ounces = 180 mL
16 tablespoons = 1 cup = 8 fluid ounces = 240 mL

Recipe Notes

Recipe Notes

Recipe Notes

Recipe Notes